Building
Value
to Last

Building Value to Last

Crystal Maggelet

President and CEO of FJ Management

with Sarah Ryther Francom and Laura Best Smith

GIBBS SMITH
TO ENRICH AND INSPIRE HUMANKIND

First Edition
23 22 21 20 19   5 4 3 2 1

Published by
Gibbs Smith
P.O. Box 667
Layton, Utah 84041
1.800.835.4993 orders
www.gibbs-smith.com

Designed by Sky Hatter
Cover design by Virginia Snow
Printed and bound in China

Gibbs Smith books are printed on either recycled, 100% post-consumer waste, FSC-certified papers or on paper produced from sustainable PEFC-certified forest/controlled wood source. Learn more at www.pefc.org.

Names: Maggelet, Crystal, 1964- author. | Francom, Sarah Ryther, 1982-
    author. | Smith, Laura Best, 1961- author.
Title: Building value to last / Crystal Maggelet with Sarah Ryther
    Francom and Laura Best Smith.
Description: First edition. | Layton, Utah : Gibbs Smith, [2019] |
Includes bibliographical references and index.
Identifiers: LCCN 2018039577 | ISBN 9781423640127 (hardcover : alk. paper)
Subjects: LCSH: Flying J (Firm) | Truck stops--North America. | Maggelet,
    Crystal, 1964-
Classification: LCC TL153 .M33 2018 | DDC 338.7/6655092 [B] --dc23
LC record available at https://lccn.loc.gov/2018039577

Contents

The Start of a Family Business

Principle: Treating customers right, hard work, and determination lead to entrepreneurial success.

I remember the exact moment I feared for Flying J's future. Just one week before Christmas 2008, I answered my cell phone and heard that the company my father had built over the past 50 years was on the brink of bankruptcy. I never saw it coming. I was in shock.

Flying J was a billion-dollar company, named one of *Forbes*'s largest private companies. We had just come off some of the best years we'd ever had. How could this be happening?

From that second on, my life as I knew it was over. I had been a stay-at-home mom, caring for my four young children. Though I was serving on the Flying J Board of Directors at the time, my involvement in the family business was limited. But now a problem—and an opportunity—landed right in my lap. Flying J was about to file for Chapter 11 bankruptcy. We owed billions of dollars to thousands of creditors. Our longtime CEO and president would soon depart from the company. Was I up to the challenge of leading Flying J out of this tumultuous period?

I am Crystal Maggelet, daughter of Flying J founder Jay Call, and president and CEO of FJ Management, the company that emerged from Flying J's bankruptcy. After three weeks in bankruptcy the current CEO resigned his position. I was asked by the remaining executive team to take his place and hopefully save my dad's company from complete ruin.

This book is about my life journey growing up as the daughter of two entrepreneurs, getting my education, starting a business, getting married, raising a family, and running our family business.

My story would likely have been very different if my dad had not been born to Osborne and Janice Call in 1942. Osborne was born at the turn of the twentieth century in the rugged western frontier that today is Star Valley, Wyoming. With no close business role models, no ready source of capital, and no formal education on how to start and operate a business, Osborne amassed a petroleum and car sales business that posted significant annual sales throughout the 1950s.

Osborne was a dealmaker with few equals. The first major hurdle for a budding entrepreneur is to acquire backing or capital. Osborne's uncanny ability to envision and negotiate barter arrangements with suppliers and property owners eliminated his need to put cash up front on many of his business endeavors. As soon as the ground was broken for one gas station, he was exchanging construction materials and services for the future delivery of gas. Using this approach he cut down on required capital and locked in customers. When he owned an automobile agency, he swapped an associate a new car in exchange for a local building. As owner of a motel, he arranged a similar fuel barter agreement with the company providing laundry service. And as was quite often his practice, he purchased choice property in Rupert, Idaho, with a new pickup as a down payment.

Another of Osborne's winning characteristics was the length he would go to acquire and please customers. When a lumber truck was driving through town, he jumped into his pickup with a gas tank on the back, followed the driver to his camp 15 miles into the mountains, and promptly sold him the load of fuel.

Osborne also had a congenial, friendly personality. Jolly, gregarious, and fun loving, he was liked by everyone. More than once after delivering a car to Salt Lake City and arranging for a ride home, he would sell his host a new automobile by the time he got home to Soda Springs, Idaho. Customers came back year after year, enchanted by Osborne's personality even if they still questioned whether he had given them a good deal on their purchases. (Howard M. Carlisle, *Colonist Fathers, Corporate Sons*, 1996, p. 112.)

My dad, Jay, was Osborne's first-born son. Growing up in the small rural community of Soda Springs, Idaho, the second oldest of five children, Jay was expected to help his mother manage the household and care for his siblings while his father focused on building a car dealership and a group of gas stations. Like many young families with an entrepreneurial breadwinner, Osborne's family didn't have much in the beginning. They lived in a small home in a humble community. They scrimped with every penny and stretched every morsel of food. Osborne's frugality was extreme and at times unnecessary, but he was committed to doing whatever it took in business and at home to make something of himself.

Jay showed similar ambitions from a very young age, always on the lookout for a new and exciting opportunity. Fred Baugh, a family friend, recalls an encounter with young Jay: "I pulled into the service station and before the car even stopped here comes this young kid out of the service station building and puts the hose and the nozzle in my tank, starts filling and comes over to my window and says, 'Can I fill it up?' I said, 'Sure.' The next thing comes out is a rag and the cleaning bottle of water, and he went clear around all the windows on my car and had them cleaned. I have never had service like that before and that got my attention."

Like his father, Jay's ultimate goal was to build his own company. Because his father owned an automobile dealership, Jay was lucky to have regular access to a car and plenty of gas. Like most teens, the car was his ticket to freedom and popularity. But for Jay the car was more—it was an opportunity to begin building his own business. During his spare time Jay delivered fuel to farmers. He later spent his summers and weekends pumping gas, detailing cars, running errands, and selling cars.

As a high school student, Jay focused more on work and play than a formal education. He didn't see the benefit of memorizing facts and passing tests. He realized at a young age that being able to work with people would be the key to his success. With a quick wit and natural charm, he was popular among his classmates and nicknamed the "James Dean of Soda Springs."

That's not to say that Jay didn't have his share of quirks. My father was obsessed with cleanliness. His car sparkled and his clothes and shoes were always clean. He viewed cleanliness as a mark of a man in control of his life, and he even expected his friends to be clean before setting a foot in his car.

After graduating high school, my dad felt the urge to venture out on his own. He left the family home the moment he could for Provo, Utah, where he spent his first college year at Brigham Young University. But business—not education—was his real ambition. After his first year at BYU, Jay took his father up on an opportunity to manage a service station in Jackson Hole, Wyoming, during the summer break. Known as Jay's Cut Rate, the four-pump station excelled under my father's leadership. His charm and attention to customer service and cleanliness created loyal customers. Before long the Jackson Hole station was one of Osborne's most profitable stations.

That summer wasn't all work and no play. Shortly after he arrived in Jackson Hole, Jay met his first real love, Teddy Lou Brown. A young beauty with a quick wit and ambitions of her own, Jay quickly fell head over heels. Teddy, who was still a high school student in Idaho, worked as a waitress at a nearby drugstore for the summer. Jay courted Teddy over breakfasts and by the end of the summer she was his. But summer ended too quickly and Teddy left both Jackson Hole and my dad behind to return to school.

Jay felt lost without Teddy. He wanted her by his side and was used to getting what he wanted. He never returned to BYU, but instead enrolled in Idaho-based Ricks College to be closer to his summer fling. Just a few months later in 1960, immediately following Teddy's high school graduation, Teddy and Jay were married.

The newlyweds spent their first summer together managing the Jackson Hole service station. Osborne left the station completely in Jay's hands, agreeing to split the net profits fifty-fifty. Starting with only $50 to their name, the young couple was determined to turn their $50 into $100 and then into $200.

Jay and Teddy worked long, tiring hours during their first few months at the station. They were poor, young, and naïve. Jay's parents had given the couple a used 28-foot trailer to live in. It was so small, Jay and Teddy joked that they could shower, use the toilet, and brush their teeth at the same time. The trailer was parked next to the station, so Jay could see customers come in and have his dinner at the same time. Their first year together was physically rewarding and reaffirmed to both of them that hard work and determination would take them far in their future endeavors.

After recognizing Jay's talent and innate business sense, Osborne offered his son a new challenge of running the underperforming Willard, Utah, service station under the Maverik brand. Since Jay wasn't interested in finishing college and wanted to be an independent entrepreneur, he told him he would only go to Willard if his dad would agree to eventually sell him the station. The agreement was worked out and my parents packed up their belongings and made their way to the small town located at the northern end of Utah's Wasatch Front.

Jay knew he could turn the failing station around from the moment he stepped into it. My parents again parked their trailer next to the station and went to work. Jay focused on improving customer service and cleanliness—attributes that would become the foundation of my dad's business approach throughout his career.

Jay didn't just manage the four-pump station while in Willard; he sought new opportunities to grow the company even further. Within a few short weeks my dad spotted a new opportunity in a nearby trucking company whose truckers fueled up at a competing station several miles away. Jay didn't hesitate to walk right up to the trucking company's owner and pitch him a deal. Jay's goal was to get those trucks fueling at his station. Baffled but impressed by Jay's tenacity, the trucking company owner agreed to make the deal happen. From that moment on, the Willard service station offered round-the-clock service and guaranteed lower prices for the truckers. In his early twenties at the time, Jay created his first big win and officially began his relationship with the trucking industry.

My parents worked night and day, barely making a profit. But they knew their work would pay off—and it did. The Willard station's business began growing, at a much faster pace than Osborne expected. During the first few months the station's sales were roughly 500 gallons a day. By midsummer the station's sales had doubled to a thousand gallons a day, and in just a few more months sales had tripled. Jay and Teddy had succeeded. But like any true entrepreneur, my dad was not satisfied with what he had accomplished. He never stopped searching for more opportunities to become more successful.

After three years running the Willard station, the once-failing site had become Osborne's largest volume outlet. It was clear that Jay had the leadership, tenacity, and foresight needed to be successful in business. Osborne kept his word and sold the station to Jay at fair market value. Not long after that, on August 14, 1964, I entered the world. Unfortunately, Osborne died of a heart attack just three weeks later on September 7.

My dad didn't speak much of his father's death, but I imagine it profoundly affected him. Osborne showed Jay by example that anyone could accomplish anything if they truly wanted to. Osborne never cut corners, nor did he shy away from a risky opportunity. He was honest, dedicated, and determined. Though Osborne's business never grew to the scale of what my father would accomplish, in many ways Osborne paved the way for what my father was to build.

Osborne's passing created a void in Caribou Four Corners, the fuel group owned by Osborne and his brother Reuel, which became a serious management crisis. The brothers had merged their fuel companies just six months earlier, and much of the business was still being consolidated. By combining their holdings, the brothers had hoped to become significant players in the retail petroleum industry in a four-state area. By spreading out geographically they were less vulnerable to a business downturn in one area or the dominance of a strong local competitor.

The merger had created a large enterprise comprising two refineries and expanding retail and wholesale operations, including more than 60 retail outlets. The company needed an executive team that had experience and expertise. With Osborne's passing, Reuel knew he couldn't do it alone. Reuel wanted to keep the company intact, and although Jay was young, Reuel considered his nephew to be confident, aggressive, inquisitive, and a quick learner. Of more importance, he was a self-starter and willing to make the personal sacrifices necessary to tenaciously ramrod new projects into being.

Although my dad proved to have an innate business sense, a solid work ethic, and high ambitions, he simply lacked the years of experience required to be considered a bona fide business executive. He was only 24 at the time of his father's death. Yet Reuel felt inspired by his nephew's talents and mindset, and offered Jay a role as vice president in the Caribou Four Corners business.

My father was reluctant to accept Reuel's offer. When Caribou Four Corners was originally founded only eight months earlier, Jay had purposely declined to merge his Willard station into the company. He had feared it would inhibit his own plans. Still, Reuel's offer was tempting. My father had always looked up to Reuel. Uncle and nephew had many things in common, and not just in the business realm—they also both shared a passion for flying airplanes. Moreover, Jay had long considered Reuel his favorite uncle, and Reuel felt similarly about Jay. Acknowledging that joining Caribou Four Corners was another learning opportunity, Jay decided to join his uncle.

For the next three years my dad worked for Caribou Four Corners. He protected the stock interest his mother still had in the company and learned about the industry from his uncle Reuel, managing several stations and opening new properties. Reuel was an influential role model throughout Jay's early career. In many ways Reuel showed Jay the ins and outs of operating a large business with several entities. My dad's responsibilities were diverse, including overseeing stations, collecting major overdue accounts, and advertising locations. It was during his three short years at Caribou Four Corners that my dad was able to learn and grasp the multitude of responsibilities it takes to manage a large business.

Reuel and Jay Call, both pilots, posing with the corporate plane, ca. 1965.

While working alongside his uncle, Jay also acquired stations of his own. He eventually had four stations in four western states: in Willard, Utah; Ontario, Oregon; Lewiston, Idaho; and Barstow, California. A key to my dad's early success was his focus on volume over high profit margins. Lines of cars wrapped around his Fastway stations waiting to pump lower-priced fuel. At nearly half the price of local competitors, Jay's stations sold more fuel resulting in higher revenues. But my father was still restless, and with each passing month he grew more anxious to branch out completely on his own. By February 1968, Jay and Reuel parted ways and my dad officially launched his own company, Flying J. It was one of his proudest moments—one that he had worked to achieve nearly his entire life up to that point. Those early acquisitions, which Jay financed with his personal earnings and bank loans, blazed the trail for the giant organization Flying J would one day become.

The Happiest Childhood

Principle: Learn to accept change and make the most of it.

The Perfect Family—Brigham City, Utah

'm told I came into the world as a demanding, crying baby. I prefer to say that I was impatient and couldn't wait for life to start. Ultimately it was discovered that the medications my mother's doctor put her on had affected my development, so when I was separated from my mother I actually had to go through drug withdrawal. Regardless of how it started, I was ready to tackle my life from day one.

My parents ran a true mom-and-pop operation. My dad would find promising locations and build a station. My mom would then order the fuel, do the business books, and handle advertising for the station. If a motel was involved, my mom handled the room decorating, facility staffing, and room bookings. My dad would call home every night and they would discuss the problems of the day and make the appropriate business plans for the following day. Our house was literally the office during the weekdays and turned back into a home on the weekends, when my parents didn't talk about work.

By the time I'd come along, my brother, Thad, was already two years old. As we got older, the mom-and-pop plan didn't work any longer. Thad and I were becoming more demanding and the company had grown to 15 stations. Though my parents made a great business team, it was time to move into a regular home and hire company employees. My dad took over managing the business, while my mom transitioned to managing our social and family lives.

Jay adopted many operational strategies that he had learned from his father and uncle Reuel—strategies that led to significant cost savings and growth. Reuel had developed a consignment scheme that proved to be beneficial for station operators. Instead of employing station managers, Jay attracted operators by offering them free rent in on-site trailers and basing earnings on the amount of fuel sold. Because operators lived on-site and had a vested interest, there was more incentive to take ownership over the station, which meant better customer service and higher sales. During Flying J's first several years, this model proved to be a win-win scenario for Jay and the operators.

Rather than slowing down, my mother started volunteering in the school and community. She worked in the PTA, joined a social sorority called Beta Sigma Phi, and ran the local Heart Fund Drive for Box Elder County in Utah. Being versed in working deals, she was able to raise double the money by talking her sorority into hosting a Valentine's ball with the proceeds going to the local Heart Fund. I

Crystal, Teddy, Jay, and Thad in front of a friend's home in Washington taken on one of the family's cross-country trips, ca. 1973.

remember how proud of her I was when she won the coveted Queen of Hearts Award from the American Heart Association for her work in Utah. There was even an article written on her in the local paper. Her level of energy and commitment to people was impressive, and as busy as she stayed, I never felt neglected. She was always there for me and my brother. She was smart and beautiful and all my friends were jealous because they wanted a mom like mine.

Although my dad was not home much, when he *was* around he had a huge presence. I couldn't ask for a more loving and physically affectionate dad. I remember at a young age jumping off the countertop into his arms for a big hug. When we were together on the weekends, especially when we were camping, he was very attentive, fishing, motorbiking, and playing games with us. We knew we were loved, but he was very independent and liked to be able to do what he wanted when he wanted, which did not always work with young kids around. Aside from going on fun outings and being at family dinners a few times a week, my dad wasn't much of a family man.

We lived in a small neighborhood, where I enjoyed tagging along with my older brother. I gained the reputation of a tattletale, and I often felt alone and left behind. When I started school, my lonesome life didn't get much better. I was extremely uncoordinated and was always chosen last for kickball games. Fortunately I made a few close friends during my elementary years that helped make my shy existence bearable. I found the most peace and comfort on our family weekend camping adventures or at our Monday night dinners, before my dad left town each week on business.

From an early age, I understood our family was a bit different from most of the families in Brigham City, Utah. I attended Mountain View Elementary, where many of the kids' parents were teachers at Intermountain Indian School or worked at Thiokol, a large aerospace and chemical manufacturing company that employed several thousand people. I knew my parents were building a business. Listening to them talk over dinner, I also believed it was going well and that their hard work was paying off. Our family was living the American dream. There were lots of sacrifices along the way, such as a dad that was not home many nights a week, but I did not know any different, so I had a happy childhood. I always thought we were the perfect family of four—Mom, Dad, my big brother, and me; or at least that's what I'd learned from watching television. As I recall, most commercials had a mom, dad, sister, and brother. Our family just seemed very balanced and happy. Our home was small and humble, but to me we always had a great life with more than we needed—more than most other families like ours.

Thad and I both enjoyed school. We loved to learn. However, it didn't take me long to realize that Thad did little studying or prep work and easily passed classes with high grades, whereas I had to study hard for every class. In fact, it wasn't until I was in the third grade that an attentive teacher noticed that I wasn't learning to read but instead was memorizing all the words in a story and merely repeating what I memorized. This Brigham City teacher volunteered her time two or three days after school to work one-on-one with me until I learned how to read phonetically. If that teacher hadn't taken an interest in me at that time I am certain I would have had a very different life. Once I got reading down, I took off.

Watching my mother organize our social life taught me how to plan. In fact, in elementary school I not only knew which friends were coming over for the weekend sleepover, but had assigned them what to bring, which dolls we would be playing with, and what we would eat. In high school, I was the designated group organizer and planner. I'm certain I learned this from watching the active social life of my mother. She was very outgoing and had tons of friends. She was a farm girl who married two weeks after her high school graduation, but similar to my father she was extremely ambitious and independent.

My dad wasn't just ambitious, he was also innovative. Beyond fuel, his service stations began selling groceries. Though selling groceries and food is now commonplace at a local gas station, at the time of Flying J's launch, the convenience store model was practically nonexistent.

In its first five years, Flying J built 23 new stations: nine in California, eight in Washington, five in Oregon, and one in Nevada. Flying J had officially taken off, and my dad remained at the controls, guiding his company through the ups and downs of the often turbulent business world.

When I was eight, my family moved from our small, humble home to one of the biggest houses in Brigham City. Our neighborhood was known as "Snob Hill." Now I not only had my own bedroom, but a bathroom shared with my brother, and a whirlpool hot tub in the basement. It was a big change for all of us. The house established us as a family that had made it. We were now known at school as the "rich kids." As I recall, it would mostly happen when I was picked up by the bus and kids would comment that we were the kids from Snob Hill. I am not sure at the time that I really even knew if they were talking about me or just all of us neighborhood kids. I knew we had a nice life, but I thought all our neighbors were rich.

However, just like every family, no matter how perfect we looked from the outside, we had our share of troubles. My dad was gone a lot. It wasn't that he left early and worked late—he was gone Tuesday through Friday, most every week. My mom would send him off right, with a warm, home-cooked meal every Monday night. My mom was a great cook. We'd spend those nights before his departure at the kitchen table, enjoying plates of meat and potatoes, talking about our plans for the week. And then, just like that, my dad would take off in his small plane bound for the West Coast, where the majority of the Flying J business was located to avoid competing with his uncle Reuel.

When the weekend finally came and my dad was home, my parents took advantage of it. We were always on the move. Our family of four would jump in our four-wheel-drive Vista Liner camper or later our motor home and escape for a weekend of great fishing and nighttime card games. Once in a while we would even get to travel in my dad's plane to faraway places like SeaWorld or Disneyland, where I felt privileged to stay at a Motel 6. We never stayed in those fancy resort hotels. They were way too expensive for our family, according to my very frugal dad. In my eyes our life was still luxurious. None of my friends flew anywhere, especially in their own family plane.

I was nine years old when I first knew something was wrong in my family. Almost until the day my parents divorced they acted like newlyweds—flirting, kissing, and hugging. Though I rarely saw my parents fight, I could sense a growing tension in our home. My parents cried a lot and there was lots of whispering. They both lost weight and neither seemed happy anymore. Their unhappiness caught me by surprise. We had just moved into our big, new, beautiful home, the business seemed to be doing well, and we were having many small family adventures. I had not been exposed to marriages falling apart and had no idea my parents' marriage was about to collapse, but within a few months my parents divorced.

I took their divorce hard. The life that I knew was upended before I could grasp what was happening. My family—my picture-perfect family—was breaking into pieces. The years of my dad traveling every week had been a huge sacrifice and my parents had grown apart. They had created separate lives and did not know how to bring the pieces back together. My dad sat Thad and me down and told us that he was moving out, and he wasn't going to force us to spend time with him. He would make himself available if we wanted to see him, but *we* would have to call *him*—he would not reach out to us. And just like that he was gone.

Every few months we would reach out to him and he would come, as promised. He always made an effort to see us when we called, even if he had to fly to pick us up. He was a firm believer that parents and children should have their own lives independent of one another. Family times should be special and infrequent so they were more meaningful and so that family members did not take each other for granted or live vicariously through one another. We would spend weekends together at his home in Brigham City, or he would fly us to his condo in Palm Springs for a few days. It was always an adventure, not just a quick bite or a movie.

His new wife, Tamra, was always kind to us, and we were introduced to a number of her hobbies, like raising llamas and trying

Crystal, Thad, and Jay board a King Air jet piloted by Jay for one of many trips to stay in Palm Springs, California, ca. 1978.

new cuisine. She was an amazing cook and a gracious hostess. One time he took us to Mexico and another time to Hawaii. The times with my dad were always fun, but the adventures weren't the same without my mom and the time with my dad was never long enough. Like many children, I directed my frustration toward the closest person to me—my mom. I resented the way my life had drastically changed, and I often lashed out at her for not supporting me, as well as for other stupid problems that at the time seemed of dire consequence.

Our relationship didn't get any better when she started working outside the home after the divorce. She had a newfound energy and was starting a new and very different life for herself. I hated it. Though Thad and I were 13 and 11 years old, I resented that she was leaving us to fend for ourselves. I missed having my mom at home now and I didn't understand why I was no longer a big part of her life. I found myself sharing my mom with her new boyfriends, her new hobbies, and her demanding job.

My mom joined a girlfriend in a clothing business venture. Opening a clothing store called Reaggae Women in Salt Lake City was just the therapy she needed. She found her calling quickly running the sophisticated high-end shop for working women. I watched my mom gain her self-worth back as she traveled to San Francisco and Los Angeles purchasing clothing and jewelry for her upscale clientele. She didn't make a lot of money during this venture, but she was the best-dressed mom around!

Though this job was therapeutic for my mom, it was frustrating for me. I tagged along when she went to work just so I could be close to her, but it was extremely boring. You'd think as a young girl I would love such a place, but I hated it. I was still frustrated with her and let her know it. I felt forced to kill time while my mom worked, but subliminally I was learning how to work with the public through my mom's skillful abilities in sales.

My mom tried to balance kids, work, and dating. I'm sure she did the best she could, and though she only worked Tuesdays and Saturdays, as a kid it seemed like she was always gone. I was miserable because my picture-perfect family life was over. I promised myself then and there that I would never leave my kids to selfishly go to work.

On the Move—Rexburg, Idaho

I was 13 years old when my mom told me she was getting remarried and we were moving to Rexburg, Idaho. I wasn't upset, since some of my happiest memories were spending time at my grandparents' Idaho farm. I felt comfortable there. Idaho, in many ways, was already my second home. I was excited to move to a different town, where we would have a new start.

Rexburg was the perfect place to be a carefree teen. Like many teenagers, my life revolved around my friends. My class at Madison Junior High only had 200 kids and I loved it. I made lots of friends and loved the small-town feel. I was able to get an Idaho driver's license at age 14 and Mom bought me a car. I could drive until sunset, so I spent many weekend evenings dragging Main Street. I was on the drill team and obsessed with boys. I also became very active in the local LDS church (Church of Jesus Christ of Latter-day Saints). The warmth of the community enveloped me, and for the first time in several years I felt like I had a normal family and life.

One of my happiest memories was the fall potato harvest. Students were released from school for two weeks to work in Idaho's famous potato fields. It was a critical time for the farmers to bring in their main potato crop before it froze. Hooked behind a tractor, the harvester was a big yellow machine with chain conveyor belts that dug potatoes out of the ground as it noisily lumbered up each row. As the potatoes and dirt moved up the conveyor belt, dirt fell between the chains. Standing on a small platform, we picked vines and debris from the potatoes before they fell into a hopper to be bagged into a 30-pound burlap sack. The work was tedious, and at the end of the day both face and clothes were caked with dirt. Though it was dirty and exhausting work, I looked forward to those two weeks every year and learned what it felt like to work hard and be rewarded with a well-earned paycheck. It was also a time when I saw great collaboration among the farmers, their full-time workers, temporary workers, and teens. Everyone pitched in to get the harvest done in a timely manner. Although it was fun, I knew it was not how I wanted to spend my adult years—doing hard labor. I began to understand why my mom had wanted to leave the farm, where it was incredibly hard manual work for little financial gain.

My mom's new husband was everything my dad wasn't. He was easygoing, passive, and had zero ambition. He was just there. My mom thought it would be best to marry someone who was the polar opposite of my dad, and she got it. However, she was bored with him even before we finished unpacking. My mom was accustomed to more action than the little town of Rexburg offered—she needed to be busy; she needed a job.

My mom, though unhappy in her second marriage, excelled at her own business during our time in Idaho. About 1979 she got to know a couple that ran Diet Center. When they saw how business savvy my mother was, they offered her the Dallas/Fort Worth territory of the Diet Center business. Though we were still living in Idaho, she packed her bags and set off for Dallas to learn the ropes. I don't know why she thought she could sell and manage the franchises, but she wasn't afraid and needed a challenge in her life. Her 15-year education running a business with my dad and starting her dress store gave her the self-confidence she needed. My mother understood what it was like to be a working mother. Her gut instincts told her Diet Center would be a great business for women who wanted not only to raise their kids but to have a career outside the home. With this in mind, Teddy took the initiative and purchased one of the franchises to come up with a model of her own. She rented a spot in a commercial building and hired a manager, who coincidently wanted to lose 15 pounds. The manager lived in an affluent neighborhood where her friends watched her successfully lose weight. She opened the center and was an overnight success. In less than six months she had 60 dieters.

This model helped others see the vision, and Teddy began selling franchises within her territory to others. She had been right, and within only a few years she was providing opportunities for many women in a time that did not offer many career options for them.

Since much of my mom's business was in Texas, she traveled frequently, and I spent several summer breaks traveling with her. At the time, I thought her business was incredibly boring, but if it meant that the only way I could see her was to travel with her, I went. As the seemingly endless business meetings dragged on, I began watching how easily my mom motivated her employees. There was a reason her Diet Center franchises were taking off so quickly, and she was it—her employees loved her. As I grew older, the resentment I felt toward my mother slowly evolved into admiration.

Over the next four years my mother amassed 20 Diet Centers. She even talked her mother into helping her run the centers. My grandmother had no experience working outside the home other than helping my grandfather with his farm, but she quickly learned how to best support my mom. She taught herself how to type, do clerical work, professionally answer the phone, and keep the business organized as it grew. This was amazing to watch, since my memories of my grandmother were helping her make bread and picking raspberries together. She was an amazing homemaker, but watching my grandmother take on a new challenge and excel at it further demonstrated how much courage the women in my life had. The retirement fund earnings from this job supported my grandmother until her death at 98. By the time my grandfather died she had become a self-sufficient, independent woman supporting herself. This was especially impressive to me considering she was born in 1920, the year women were first able to vote, and married at a very young age.

Her ambition, friendly demeanor, and love for entertaining also meant that she invited the most interesting people over for dinner. In the beginning they were mostly social friends. She always hosted a Christmas party and other events. She had many friends and business associates through her Diet Center business. Later when she was dating, the men she would bring home were helpful and interesting to me. Most were college educated, and I was in high school with little exposure to college graduates. I learned very early that if I behaved and acted like an adult I would be treated like one. I don't remember ever being asked to leave if I wanted to stay. I really enjoyed talking to adults about their lives and trying to learn from them.

Through my teen years I admired my mom professionally. But I still felt the scars from when I was 10 years old, when my mom went from being a stay-at-home mom to a working mother, an abrupt change I was not prepared for at such a tender age. In retrospect, she was there for me in so many ways. She showed me all that women can accomplish. After a devastating divorce she picked herself right back up and became an accomplished, successful businesswoman. She was an exceptional role model for me.

My years in Idaho were some of my best teen memories. But my life was again about to change. My mom filed for divorce, which meant we were leaving Idaho.

Getting an Education at School and Work

Principle: Becoming independent boosts self-confidence.

At most I had a few months left in Idaho before we moved back to Utah. The plan was to see Thad graduate from high school and we'd be on our way. I was devastated. I couldn't believe my mom was ripping me out of my home again. I ignored her early warnings and enjoyed my final days in Idaho, refusing to acknowledge the looming move. Then the day came. I was 16 years old, just about to start my junior year, and we were moving back to Salt Lake City. "It's for the best. It'll be good for us," she said, trying to calm my anger.

Her idea of a compromise was letting me choose which high school I would attend, ultimately deciding our new neighborhood.

She gave me three options: Bountiful High School in Bountiful, Judge Memorial High School in Salt Lake City, or Cottonwood High School in Murray, Utah. I appreciated the involvement I was being given in the decision, but what I really wanted was to be left behind in Idaho to live with my grandparents until I finished high school. Mom told me we would both be starting new lives and it would be fun in Utah. I disagreed. There wasn't anything fun about being forced to leave an amazing life.

Begrudgingly, I checked out each of the three high schools. I well remember visiting Judge Memorial, a private Catholic school, and as a devout Mormon girl watching priests take a smoke break, I knew there was no way I was going there. Ironically, years later, three of my four children would attend and graduate from Judge Memorial.

I landed at Bountiful High School because with several Mormon kids there and the neighborhood being largely Mormon, I felt most at home. My first few months were very difficult. I did not fit in well as a country girl from Idaho, wearing the wrong clothes and ratting my hair high like Charlie's Angels. I became a different person at Bountiful High. With only a few friends and a limited social network, I focused more seriously on schoolwork.

I chose to embrace this new change instead of fight it. Instead of the drill team I joined business clubs, like DECA and Future Business Leaders of America. I was drawn to business, accounting, and marketing classes, and took the opportunity to strengthen my academic load with AP and honors classes that were not available in Idaho. I was starting to grow more serious about my future and learning about business, which is all I had seen my parents do.

On the few days a month that I saw my dad, I listened as he asked my brother how he was doing in school and hoped he would also ask me. I wanted to brag about *my* high GPA and tough classes. But he rarely inquired. He didn't seem to take much interest in who I was or what I had accomplished. His lack of interest motivated me to do more. I wanted to accomplish something that would capture his attention.

I had always worked. After babysitting and working the potato harvest, I learned I liked having my own money. When I moved to Utah, I asked my dad if I could work at one of his convenience stores. He told me no—because I was a girl. That made me mad, so I worked at the McDonald's restaurant in the local mall for nearly two years instead. I also worked because I wanted to be independent. I wanted to make something of myself and show that I wasn't depending on my family's success. I enjoyed my time at McDonald's and realized I liked working with others and learning new things. When I had to quit, my manager insisted I keep my uniform, hoping I would return and work there again. I'm a bit sentimental, and in fact I still have that uniform. (I wonder if McDonald's would hire me back today?)

My dad invited Thad and me to Flying J's grand openings. It was exhilarating to be part of his accomplishments. In Utah, people—even kids my age—knew the Flying J brand. As I drove by stations and saw billboards, I would think with pride, "That's my dad's business." I was so proud to be part of something big and know that it was my family's legacy. I also continued to watch my mother inspire women to successfully develop their own Diet Center franchises. She eventually helped develop 36 Diet Center franchises in Texas.

By the time I graduated from high school I was proud of what my parents had accomplished and I wanted to be just like them. I began to see how their ambition and accomplishments were unique from my friends' parents. They were paving their own paths. Flying J and Diet Center were both growing, and I had more reason than ever to take pride in my family's businesses.

Living through my parent's divorce I recognized how easy it was to make life-changing mistakes at an early age. More than anything, I did not want to get divorced. In many ways, staying happily married was my top priority. My mother got married at 18, right out of high school. My dad wasn't much older. He was 20 years old when they tied the knot.

"Don't do what I did. Wait until you have a college education before getting married," my mom would say over and over to me. She was not the only one reinforcing this concept. Because our home was always swarming with adults that my mom had invited over, it gave me the unique opportunity to seek advice and learn from their experiences. I viewed adults as a treasure chest of information.

"What would you do differently?" I'd repeatedly ask adults. The advice was always the same:

"Don't get married young."

"Go to school. Graduate college."

"Wait until you're at least 21 before getting married."

Those invaluable, somewhat simple words reinforced within me what I already knew—that I was going to go to college and I wasn't going to jump into marriage. I wanted to absorb as many experiences as I could.

Putting marriage aside, my first step was college and I felt ready. Going to college was never a question for me. There was no debate or thought about it—college was what you did after high school. Beyond that, however, I had no idea where life would take me. I studied business because it was all I had seen and it was familiar and comfortable to me. Since neither of my parents and very few of my relatives had completed college, I am not certain where this burning desire came from. Perhaps I saw it as a way to set myself apart from my very successful parents—to make a name for myself by doing something neither of them had done.

By the time I entered college, I had grown to become an independent, I-can-do-anything kind of girl. But like most high school kids I didn't have a clue. I lacked direction. I knew I wanted to get good grades, because I did not know where I would be going and I wanted to have an exemplary academic record that could help me do whatever I aspired to in the future. I applied to several schools and was accepted to Pepperdine University in California and Utah State University (USU) in nearby Logan, Utah, where I received an academic scholarship. With a scholarship in hand, I decided to attend USU. I was proud of myself for working hard during high school and giving myself an opportunity to pay a solid portion of my tuition costs all on my own.

Some people thought I was crazy. They thought I should start at Pepperdine. I disagreed. Why should I spend thousands of dollars on tuition costs when I could go to USU and get my general education for free? I suppose it was a sign that I had the Call frugality gene, but in reality it simply made sense.

I had a plan for how I could get through school and still do all I wanted on the smallest budget possible. After finishing my general

Alpha Chi Omega sorority sisters Crystal and Suzette Summers as Utah State freshmen, fall 1982.

education courses, I would transfer to Pepperdine or another university. I went to USU and I fell in love with it. I became completely immersed in the college life. I loved everything about Utah State. I joined a sorority and became pledge president. I also participated in student government. Even though I was a short-timer, I was fully committed to USU. I became so involved that I was one of five finalists for Female Student of the Year after my sophomore year.

My first real adventure outside of the Utah bubble was Semester at Sea, a college program that was exactly what it sounded like—a semester at sea, traveling from country to country. Together with about 400 other students from all over the United States, we boarded a ship and set sail. We spent 14 days at sea. I had anticipated learning about the world, but I was soon surprised about how much I would learn about my fellow classmates from all over the United States. They weren't like the kids I was used to. They were rich and spoiled rotten. I always knew I was privileged, but I had hoped I wasn't like them. Not very many kids can afford to do something like Semester at Sea, so it made a bit of sense that there would be several who would feel entitled. I was in shock about how many had the goal of partying or shopping around the world. One thing I was sure of was that I did not want to be like many of them. Luckily for me, by the time we reached Japan, our first stop, I had made friends who became my traveling companions for the rest of the trip.

Semester at Sea was eye opening. I loved walking the ship's deck and looking at the stars in the night sky. I went out one night to gaze at the sky and noticed that the Big Dipper in relation to the North Star was upside down! Only then did I realize how far away from home I really was. Knowing that my family was literally on the other side of the world made me homesick.

After Semester at Sea, I attended Pepperdine for two semesters. Since I only spent two semesters there, I didn't claim the school as

Crystal at the Egyptian pyramids while studying abroad during Semester at Sea, fall 1984.

mine. I was a Utah State Aggie. But Pepperdine claimed *me*. During the graduation ceremony I listened as the speakers congratulated us on all that we had accomplished. Next up they were to honor Pepperdine's most exemplary students. As I listened, I recognized the credentials they were describing—the student sounded just like me. I was called onto the stage as salutatorian of the graduating class. It was a shocking moment, since no one had told me of this honor until I was called to the stage. It was an awkward moment, being honored at another school for my accomplishments at USU. But it was still gratifying to be acknowledged for what I had achieved.

After graduating from Pepperdine, I left California to make my mark in the working world. Working was not new to me. In addition to working during high school, Dad had put me to work in a clerical job at Flying J during my college years at USU. And as a summer job, I had marketed a water park that my dad had just built.

Armed with a college degree and plenty of work experience for someone my age, I was ready to face the real world. The only problem I had—and it was a *big* problem—was that I had no idea what I wanted to do, or *could* do. Like most recent college graduates, I was lost. I did what many young college grads do: moved back in with Mom. I had graduated a semester early and felt that I had extra time to figure out what to do. It was the first time in several years that I wasn't working toward something. I wasn't doing anything.

During my college years, my brother at age 20 had married his best friend, Laurie, and was working for my dad. Video rentals were the fad and people were renting videos from different venues to watch at home. Though my mom disapproved, my dad suggested Thad manage a video rental business out of the Flying J stations. Thad didn't want to let Dad down, and knowing that my dad had not finished college and was doing fine, he took my dad up on his offer and dropped out of college in his junior year.

A few months into my job search after college graduation, my dad grew tired of my slacker lifestyle. He called me one day and said unless I had something better, "You need to come to work. Be here on Monday." I knew he wasn't messing around. My days of relaxation were over.

My dad gave me an opportunity to work in Flying J's Supply and Distribution Department. I managed our fleet of tank cars and bought and sold our liquefied petroleum gas products for our North Salt Lake Refinery. Here I was, a 22-year-old college graduate, working with primarily men who were twice my age and only a few women. What an opportunity he had given me. I was traveling across the country attending conventions and representing Flying J, which by that point had become a huge company. This job was my first foray into the real world and was challenging and exciting. I didn't have anything to prove, so I focused on learning my job well. I innately understood sales and negotiation, and I began perfecting these skills.

I was almost always the youngest individual and the only woman during sales meetings and conferences. I didn't know what to expect. I was incredibly naïve. I was confident that if I worked hard, watched, and listened that I could be successful. I don't really remember worrying too much about being the only woman in the room. I had seen my mother in action and she always did just fine. In fact, I noticed early on that my youth and womanhood could be an advantage if I played my cards right. Instead of letting my personal attributes interfere in the sales process, I'd spin them around until everyone *wanted* to do business with me. I quickly learned how to charm the businessmen around me. I was a woman in a man's world, but I wasn't going to let it slow me down. If they wanted to do business with Flying J, they had to work with me—there was no other option.

Another positive about working for Flying J is that occasionally my dad let me attend business meetings with him and his colleagues, bank executives, and customers. I ate it up. It was so fun and gratifying to see my dad in action. No longer did I think meetings were boring. Because of my dad's business accomplishments, I put him on a pedestal. He was building a company that people were starting to recognize and respect. But I admired my dad from afar. I craved his attention and I tried to do positive things by working hard at his company to gain his praise.

At this point I realized I was right on schedule with my life goals. I had graduated from a respected college before marriage and was now working in a large, thriving company. I looked back upon my childhood and recognized that I had become a stronger person because of the many ups and downs my family went through. In many ways I had a privileged childhood. I had everything I needed. I had everything I wanted. Though at times I was bitter toward my parents, I recognized that the challenges and changes I went through made me stronger. I learned to adapt. I learned that things can change fast—and they often *do* change. Most importantly I learned that I could survive change and typically end up in a better place and stronger for the experience.

Soaring Flying J

*Principle: Innovative
ideas pay off.*

W hile I was busy growing up, Flying J was growing right
alongside me. Through the 1970s, my dad, Jay, continued
his entrepreneurial pursuits of being an innovative
marketer and distributer of fuel. He started self-service stations on
the West Coast. He started a construction company that he kept
busy building motels during the fuel shortage in 1973. He then
built convenience stores and started his own trucking company
to haul fuel to all the stores. It was an exciting time to be part of
the company my dad was building. In 1979, two pivotal events took
place that would change the complexion of the company and put
Flying J on a road of continued growth and success—changes that
would create one of America's largest private companies.

Much of the historical information about Flying J in this chapter was adapted from *The
Flying J Story* by Howard M. Carlisle (HMC, 2002).

One was opening the first travel plaza (truck stop) in Ogden, Utah, which became an immediate success. The second happened when two of Jay's trusted executives brought him an opportunity that seemed too good to turn down. Thunderbird Resources, a fully integrated oil company that had nearly twice the sales and more than three times the assets of Flying J, was coming up for sale for somewhere between $30 million and $40 million. Thunderbird's assets included several gasoline stations spanning the Midwest and Northwest; three small refineries, one of which was closed; a natural gas processing plant; propane outlets; and a share of 60 oil and gas wells, which came with drilling rights. The acquisition was much larger than any bank would finance given Flying J's balance sheet, so it did not look promising. Jay decided to meet directly with Thunderbird's parent company and work his negotiating skills. He finessed a deal with Inter-City Gas Ltd. and purchased Thunderbird for $17.8 million on April 1, 1980. He had met his goal of becoming a fully integrated oil company consisting of Exploration and Production Divisions, a refinery, and a robust retail operation.

However, Flying J was about to face political and economic challenges that would wreak havoc on the company. By 1981, fuel demand and consumption had substantially decreased. Moreover, the country was about to enter an economic recession. Flying J began reducing inventories, adjusting prices, and strengthening its accounting and marketing. Eventually, monthly losses slowed and Flying J was able to turn a meager profit. By 1983, Flying J was forced to close its refineries, but was able to keep the Exploration and Production Divisions operating.

Though the Thunderbird acquisition proved challenging, Jay never regretted the decision, saying that it gave Flying J the necessary experience in refining, production, and exploration that it would need to propel future growth. It stretched Flying

J's resources thin and divided Jay's attention, but during this time, in addition to becoming a fully integrated oil company, he never lost sight of becoming the country's leading truck stop and travel plaza operator. During the early 1980s, the company slowly added to its travel plaza network. With the Thunderbird acquisition, the company grew from 350 employees to more than 700 overnight. The acquisition also included two truck stops and several travel plazas, including one in Boise, Idaho, that grew to be one of the company's most profitable sites. By 1984, Flying J operations were steadily improving, particularly within the Retail Division. The company had grown to include 65 gasoline stations, 28 convenience stores, seven travel plazas, seven restaurants, four motels, and a major video rental business. Retail operations accounted for 42 percent of Flying J's corporate sales. Wholesale operations, including refining and the oil and gas fields, accounted for the other 58 percent. By the mid-'80s, Flying J had fully recovered from the trials of the Thunderbird acquisition and was ready to continue its growth plan. But Jay knew that he needed an executive team who could take the company through its next growth phase.

Jay needed people who had strong and effective negotiating skills, broad vision, and a strategic risk-taking business approach. My dad began observing his executive team, ensuring that the right talent was in place. Jay's leadership style was to put the right people in the right place and then let them do what they do best. Once Jay had confidence in employees, they were on their own. He rarely meddled with his team—he wanted them to be responsible for their successes and failures. With a sound executive team in place, Jay knew that he needed to find someone who could assume the top leadership post. Though Jay would stay on as CEO and chair of the Flying J Board of Directors, he needed new talent to move the company forward.

He found what he was looking for in Phil Adams, who had joined the company's Accounting Department.

Phil quickly caught Jay's attention. Jay didn't view Phil's youth and inexperience as weaknesses. Instead, he thought he could mentor Phil to become a key leader in the company. In 1983, Jay

TOP (left to right): John Telford, Marcella Hume, Ron Brisendine, Jay Call, Stan Weeks, and Buzz Germer. BOTTOM (left to right): Jack Dailey, Ron Brisendine, Paul Brown, Buzz Germer, Jay Call, and Ron Parker.

promoted Phil to the position of vice president of retailing—a promotion that shocked many. But it was the first promotion of many that put Phil on a leadership track to CEO and president. In 1987, Phil was named executive vice president.

In the mid-'80s, Jay and his executive team realized the only way to expand Flying J further was to continue building travel plazas and growing assets. But they needed capital to finance their ambitions. Two risk-takers at heart, Jay and Phil were willing to do whatever it took to see Flying J become an even larger company.

In 1984, Jay came across an opportunity to acquire Husky's U.S. oil and gas production properties. Much like the Thunderbird acquisition, the possibility of acquiring Husky's assets was an enormous opportunity that Jay couldn't pass up. He approached RMT Properties, a subsidiary holding company created by Husky that retained the assets of its U.S. refining operations, about a possible sale. His assumption was spot on—RMT was preparing Husky's U.S. assets for a potential sale. The asking price was around $100 million, far outside of what Flying J could afford. Jay knew it was a long shot, but he wasn't ready to give up. For the next several months he quietly rolled the idea around in the back of his mind, trying to find a way to make it happen.

Husky's U.S. assets included three large refineries and a retail network of 400 dealers, which included 24 truck stops and 12 service stations. Husky's network of truck stops spanned 13 western states, making it the region's second-largest truck stop chain. Similar to the Thunderbird acquisition, Jay was particularly fascinated by the opportunity to acquire Husky's North Salt Lake Refinery, a move he knew would put Flying J on a new playing level with regional competitors. Adding Husky's three refineries and respected truck stops to the Flying J brand would be a big win, but pulling off an acquisition of this size would be an enormous, if not impossible, challenge.

The North Salt Lake Refinery.

An entire year passed without an offer from Flying J, but Jay never lost sight of the opportunity. He watched from the background, waiting for the right time to approach RMT again. And when an opportunity presented itself, my dad was ready to pounce. RMT had made a deal with another buyer, but the acquisition fell through when the buyer couldn't produce adequate capital. The loss was profound for RMT, which became desperate to find a buyer. Jay knew the timing was right, and he approached the embattled company about acquiring its truck stops. Though he also wanted the refineries, Flying J wasn't in a position to acquire all of Husky's assets. RMT didn't accept his offer—it wanted an all-or-nothing deal. Jay tried to pique its interest by adding the North Salt Lake Refinery to the list of properties he was willing to acquire, but again the company didn't bite.

Jay knew he had to be creative if this megadeal was going to happen. He decided to put a $2 million nonrefundable down payment on the table—a move that got RMT's attention. On June 5, 1985, RMT and Flying J reached a deal. Flying J would acquire

Husky's U.S. assets. The closing date was August 1. Jay knew that the real work—securing financing—was about to begin. He began flying across the country in search of a financial partner that would finance the acquisition. Bank after bank turned Jay down, including Flying J's primary banker, First Security. They all gave the same reason: Flying J was too small to make the acquisition. It was simply too risky. Jay was forced to ask for an extension to the August 1 closing date.

While Flying J was searching for acquisition capital, RMT was losing money fast. Jay presented RMT with a proposal to downsize its operations to mitigate losses. RMT executives were impressed by the plan, as well as with Jay's confidence and leadership ability. RMT entrusted Jay to begin managing the Husky assets on a fee basis with a plan that an ownership switch would occur within the coming months. Flying J began downsizing the organization as planned, hoping to shrink required working capital. Within three months, Jay and the executive team had significantly reduced operational expenses, and RMT was again impressed with what had been accomplished. RMT decided to help finance a deal with Flying J and guaranteed a revolving credit line at a major bank, with an agreement that Flying J would take over payments within 18 months. By the end of 1985, ownership transferred to Flying J— an accomplishment that propelled Flying J to becoming one of the largest fully integrated oil companies in the West.

By 1991, Phil had taken Jay's place as president of Flying J. Phil had earned Jay's confidence and trust. At this point, Jay began to transition into a consultancy role while empowering Phil's vision and leadership to move the company forward. Phil would take Flying J into a new era of growth and prosperity.

Jay and his team had devised an elaborate plan to develop or acquire a total of 250 interstate travel plazas. At the time, the company had 50 travel plazas, so adding another 200 was an ambitious goal. True to his nature, Jay was ready for the challenge, but the company had to first overcome two significant hurdles. First, Flying J lacked the capital required to build or acquire 200 additional units. Second, Flying J lacked a guaranteed fuel supply to keep the plazas operational and profitable.

The North Salt Lake Refinery acquired during the Husky acquisition was up and running, but couldn't supply enough fuel for all Flying J plazas. Flying J needed additional suppliers. The company worked to obtain long-term contracts with suppliers in outlying regions to ensure an adequate fuel supply, but it struggled to find a consistent partner. Flying J was forced to become a spot buyer, purchasing excess fuel from several refiners throughout the region. Though being a spot buyer had a cost advantage, as the excess fuel was often sold at inexpensive prices, it also came at a major disadvantage because the refiners weren't reliable sources of fuel. Flying J, if it were ever to accomplish Jay's dream of growing to 250 travel plazas and becoming the nation's largest diesel retailer, needed to secure a consistent fuel partner.

Into the mid-1990s, growth was slow but steady. Sixteen new travel plazas were under construction, but the pace wasn't fast enough for Jay and Phil—they wanted the company to achieve more. They recognized that Flying J needed a strong financial partner. In typical Jay fashion, his wheels began spinning until he had an idea. He wanted to approach petroleum companies about developing joint ventures that would support Flying J's goals. His idea was that the financial partner could supply capital and reduce Flying J's potential debt, which would lead to improved credibility and lending potential with bankers. The organization would also become a fuel partner, eliminating Flying J's status as a spot buyer.

Jay and Phil mailed out several proposals to large refining companies that needed a home for their excess diesel supply. The

A typical Flying J travel plaza built in the early 2000s.

proposal detailed the company's bold vision. Though Flying J was still far from being a national leader, it's daring acquisitions and rapid growth had caught the attention of several national companies. The first to respond to Jay and Phil's unique proposal was Conoco, Inc.

Conoco had long been one of Flying J's spot sellers, so the two organizations already had a trusted working relationship. For years Conoco had been operating at less than capacity and nearly always had excess fuel to sell. Just as Flying J needed a strong fuel and financial partner, Conoco was searching for a consistent buyer. The two companies began talking, and it quickly became clear that the companies' goals aligned. Conoco was interested in becoming an equity investor in Flying J. After further negotiations, the two companies reached a pioneering deal on January 9, 1991: a joint venture that would be known as CFJ Properties LLC.

The two companies combined their own unique assets and attributes, creating a complementary partnership. Conoco brought a wealth of oil experience and supply, as well as significant brand recognition. Flying J brought its rich network of travel plazas and ambitious goals. The fifty-fifty partnership required each company to put in $45 million, primarily in properties. The arrangement involved 33 facilities, 10 of which Conoco purchased from Flying J. Because Flying J was a skilled plaza operator, Conoco and Flying J agreed that Flying J would maintain operational control.

Industry competitors and experts were awed that Jay was able to pull off yet another huge deal. Beyond being a complementary partnership, the deal with Conoco relieved an immense amount of financial pressure that was hindering Flying J's growth. Jay finally saw his dream of building an interstate travel plaza network coming to life. The only thing slowing growth was the zoning and permitting process, but overall Flying J was well on its way to becoming the nation's leading diesel retailer.

By the early '90s, Jay had fully assumed a consultancy role in the company, leaving all major decisions up to CEO Phil Adams. Phil believed in technology as an important differentiator in the truck stop market. He charged Flying J's information system specialists with creating the company's first POS system. They approached the challenge head-on and developed a state-of-the-art system that was far ahead of competing systems.

Known as ROSS (retail operations sale system), Flying J's POS system streamlined and automated several time-consuming tasks, as well as being able to analyze sales data, highlight sales trends, and report transaction history. It was a winning platform envied by others in the transportation industry. It was also a platform that Phil thought could complement another idea he had hatched: a Flying J credit card, which would be Flying J's first foray into the financial industry.

In 1995, Flying J launched the Transportation Clearing House (TCH) fuel card. TCH was an industry-focused card that could be used at Flying J travel plazas, as well as at several other truck stops across the country. In addition to providing a new payment card, TCH was a third-party billing company with a multifaceted processing system. Its goal was to provide the industry the most cost-effective and efficient billing system in the transportation industry. Flying J had a 75 percent ownership stake in TCH, with Conoco holding the other 25 percent.

Releasing the card to its customers was a bold move—a move that put the company in head-to-head competition with Comdata, the dominant credit provider and information processor in the transportation industry at the time.

Flying J's next step into the financial industry was launching Transportation Alliance Bank (TAB). Though this move surprised many, for Phil it was the obvious next step. Founded in 1998 as an industrial loan corporation, TAB provided financial services to the transportation industry. For decades, long-haul drivers faced unique financial hurdles that TAB aimed to address. The bank's goal was to provide financial services and support for the often neglected drivers and their unique financial needs. Flying J had always been committed to easing the everyday life of the trucking owner/operator. Drivers have unique needs, and many people outside the industry simply didn't understand the diverse range of challenges they experienced. Living on the road for many days at a time is difficult. Seemingly simple tasks, like accessing food, fuel, even a restroom, can be challenging. It's difficult, if not impossible, to take an 18-wheeler through a McDonald's drive-through or find a place to rest on long stretches. Moreover, drivers often have to deal with issues like finding insurance or securing a loan from hundreds of miles away.

By recognizing opportunities long before others, Flying J had become a predominant leader in the long-haul trucking industry. By the beginning of 2000, Flying J had reached number 46 on *Forbes*'s list of the largest private corporations, and number 439 on the Hoover Institution's ranking of all private, public, and

Flying J Inc. officers and directors, Ogden, Utah, April 2002 (left to right): Buzz Germer, John Scales, Paul Brown, Phil Adams, Jim Baker, Jay Call, Ron Dejuncker, Crystal Maggelet, Barre Burgon, Thad Call, Richard Peterson, and Ron Parker.

government businesses. Over two decades the company had grown from 43 travel plazas to nearly 150 spanning the nation. Long-haul drivers could now travel throughout the country relying solely on Flying J's services.

Over the years, Flying J's goal had evolved to becoming a fully integrated oil and gas company that focused on supporting the small owner/operator trucker organization, with the ultimate goal to become the largest diesel provider in the North American market. But Phil Adams's vision for the company was actually much bigger—he wanted Flying J to eventually control freight movement across North America.

Real Life on My Own

Principle: Take on challenges even when failure is a possibility.

By the late '80s, Flying J was entering a new era, and so was I. When I reached my early twenties, I was starting to worry about the direction my life was taking. I had graduated from college and I had a steady job, but I was starting to wonder what was coming next. My career was going well, and I had a great group of friends, but I felt as though something was missing. I had met my personal goal of getting a college degree before marriage. Now I wanted to get married, since many of my friends were married and starting families. Although I was dating quite a bit and had met some incredible individuals, I could never commit and settle down. It frustrated me when friends and relatives were much quicker to ask when I was getting married or if I had a boyfriend than how work was going. I did not like this aspect of living in Utah in the mid-'80s, and I hoped if I left Utah again maybe I wouldn't feel this pressure. I didn't want to buckle under the pressure and marry someone just because it seemed like the thing to do at the time.

By the time I was 23, I knew it was time to leave Utah and try something new. During a trip to New York City, I was introduced to a nephew of one of my mother's friends, Greg Fullmer. He had recently graduated from Harvard Business School and was an investment banker in New York City. He was so enthusiastic about his experience at Harvard that he couldn't stop telling me how much he had learned and how many up-and-coming professionals were there. His passion convinced me to visit Boston and check it out for myself. I felt a rush of excitement as I stepped on the campus. How cool would it be to attend Harvard Business School? I would learn so much and be surrounded by the nation's best and brightest. I was completely intrigued.

After graduating from Pepperdine, I never thought I'd go back to school. But after seeing a potential opportunity to attend Harvard Business School, I thought that this could be the chance I needed to turn a new page and start another chapter in my life. I decided to apply to Harvard. I didn't think I'd actually get in, but I had nothing to lose. I had relatively good grades in college and decent work experience. The thought of it being my next destination was exhilarating. My mother was very supportive. A champion of women, she expressed how empowering it would be for me to graduate from Harvard Business School. When I received my acceptance letter, I couldn't have been more thrilled. Unfortunately, I had applied to attend in September 1988 but I had been deferred to September 1989. At first I was disappointed, but then I realized waiting another year with a firm plan in place would not be so bad.

I decided to continue working at Flying J. I started a new position: opening travel plazas. I spent the next several months traveling the country and hosting plaza grand openings. It was my first taste of the retail side of the business. I worked closely with the retail team, which introduced me to many different Flying J executives whom I had not met when I was working on the supply side of the business. Longtime Flying J employees helped me learn the ropes. It was a fulfilling year, during which I learned a new side of the business and became very proud of the brand we were developing across the country.

Before I knew it the year was over and I was on my way to Harvard Business School in Boston. I had never been around so many young and ambitious people—especially so many young and ambitious women. I was no longer the only one of my peers who was happy being single and career driven. I was part of an ambitious, up-and-coming generation who was preparing to take the world by storm. It was truly inspiring to be in an environment that encouraged you to work toward something more than starting a family. I found my element in Boston, and I loved it.

It was 1989, a time when career women were still confronted with enormous challenges and cultural pressures. Yet the women I was getting to know during my early days at Harvard were truly inspiring. They were hard working, determined, and self-reliant. They weren't afraid of anything. I had never been around women my age who exuded so much confidence and strength. I genuinely admired those smart, driven women. We all shared one common trait: we wanted to be successful and believed we could be. At the age of 25, I felt more independent than ever. I did not need to get married to be happy in life. Even if I were single forever I would be fine.

My first few months at Harvard were very tough academically. For the first time I was surrounded by people who were all used to being on top. Many had a much better education than I had. It was great to learn from and with them. But at the same time there was another side to being surrounded by so many talented individuals. I felt a sense of intimidation. I knew there was a real possibility that I could fail. I had always been a straight A student. I had always accomplished whatever I set my mind to. I did not believe I was the most intelligent, but I had always found success by working hard. Was hard work going to see me through this time? After a few months at Harvard, I felt inferior and questioned my ability to compete among this elite group of peers. I had never been one to worry, yet I worried. What if I fail? What then?

As a first-year business school student, I was placed in a class of 90 students. We remained together throughout all our classes, sitting in the same classroom and the same seats while the professors rotated in and out of the room. Harvard Business School relies on a pass/fail system. You either pass or you fail—there's no in-between. In every class the bottom 10 percent of students had to fail. It was inevitable—I would fail. My first semester I found myself in that failing group, being in the bottom 10 percent in one of four classes. It was a dark day for me when I received my report card. In my gut I knew that I could do better and that I would graduate from Harvard. But I couldn't help but think about the possibility of failure. What if I were at the bottom too many times?

It was intimidating and it was scary. Most of these students—including me—had never failed. We had always been at the top of our class. It was painful to fail and worrisome to think one may fail too many times to obtain a degree. I compared notes with my classmates. A few had finished the first semester with similar marks to mine. I was reassured that it would be okay, but I hoped this was just part of the process—to learn it was okay to fail. I had to get comfortable with failing and move on. I worked harder to improve my writing skills and class participation. I was determined that I would never be at the bottom of the class again, and I wasn't.

Another key aspect of my time at Harvard was its reliance on the case study learning method. In each class we would examine specific cases, propose possible solutions, and discuss outcomes. Every day we were thrown three or four different scenarios and we had to figure out what we thought should be done. Preparing each day was essential, because you were always at risk for what was called a "cold call," where you would be asked to open the case for the rest of the class. This was a shy girl from Utah's worst nightmare. I well remember the first time I was cold-called; it was a marketing case about Black & Decker. I was so obviously nervous that when I completed the opening my 90 classmates gave me a standing ovation as a show of support. In spite of my fear of public speaking, the case study method fit my learning style perfectly,

Tamra, Crystal, and Jay Call at Crystal's Harvard Business School graduation, June 1991.

and though I didn't know it at the time, would prepare me to tackle enormous challenges throughout my career. This type of training became invaluable later in my career when real life became a series of case studies.

After graduating with an MBA from Harvard, I jumped right back into the business world. I worked for a very small company called Cardmember Publishing selling telemarketing to bank credit card portfolios. I was again traveling the country, meeting with executives and pitching the product. I lived in Stamford, Connecticut, and was very close to Manhattan. Spending my days at work and my weekends in the city, I was having a blast and learning a lot of creative sales techniques. I worked with fun, smart people, and I was happy to be back in an entrepreneurial environment like Flying J.

After a few years, even though I felt I had a bright future, I was missing my family and worried I would end up settling in the East when I really wanted to be in the West long term. I began planting seeds with my western contacts, letting them know I was interested in moving back home. I also contacted my dad. I wanted him to know that I was willing to return to Utah. Though I was in no hurry to go back, I knew it was time to begin weighing my options.

My life was about to change in the fall of 1992. In October, my dad called me out of the blue.

"I have a unique opportunity I think you should consider," he said over the phone. He wanted to meet face-to-face the next time I was coming to Utah.

Coincidentally, I was planning to attend a wedding in Calgary, so I thought, "What the heck, I'll stop in Utah for a quick visit on my way home and listen to what my dad has to say." Maybe it was the opportunity I was looking for, maybe not. Regardless, I wanted to keep all doors open. Little did I know that that October weekend would change my life as I knew it.

I landed in Calgary, anxious to have a night out with my girlfriends and forget about life for a while. As we picked up our luggage, we noticed Chuck Maggelet standing alone by the baggage carousel. He seemed frustrated. "They lost my luggage," he sighed. I knew Chuck from Harvard. We had three classes together: Service Management, Real Estate, and Entrepreneurial Management. Still, he wasn't someone I knew well; only an acquaintance. And he certainly wasn't someone I wanted to spend my brief weekend in Calgary with. My friends knew Chuck better than I did and wanted to give him a ride to the hotel. I didn't see a reason to object, but I really didn't want him tagging along during our girls' night out— and he could tell. We piled into the taxi and made our way to the hotel. I breathed a sigh of relief when he caught the hint and didn't ask to come out with us.

I saw Chuck the next morning at brunch. I teased him about his lost luggage and we began to talk. When we were coincidentally seated by each other at the wedding dinner, our friends teased us that we had switched the name cards. He was so easy to talk to. We had shared common experiences growing up, had many of the same friends from school, and attended many of our school friends' weddings. We just clicked. I found myself with him the rest of the night, especially when we discovered our shared interest in partner dancing. We ended up laughing and dancing together for hours. It was a blast.

Still on a high from the wonderful time I had experienced in Calgary, I headed to Salt Lake City to meet with my dad. I was also thinking about the discussion I would have with my dad. Did he think I should move back home? Did he want me to join Flying J? Did *I* want to join Flying J? Dad never groomed Thad or me to run his business and he never articulated that he was expecting that. In fact, he would often say we should do what we wanted. However, he did many things to help us gain business experience, such as putting us on the Flying J Board of Directors at 18, and providing a small real estate company for us to run to put ourselves through college.

He met me at the airport and drove me directly to a site in down-town Salt Lake City. It was a plot of land with old buildings on it. My dad cut right to the chase. He wanted to open a hotel in Salt Lake on this site, and he was offering the opportunity to me first to build and manage the property and hotel concept. He had worked with a consulting firm to examine the probability that a hotel would work. He showed me the numbers. The study indicated that the Salt Lake market was in dire need of more hotel rooms. I didn't give it much thought before telling my dad I wanted to do it. My gut told me that this was an opportunity I couldn't pass up. I also knew that my dad rarely thought that doing one of anything that became successful made sense. If the hotel was a hit, I suspected he would want to build more under the same name and expand our lodging presence.

I knew that my dad was a hands-off leader. If I took this oppor-tunity, it would be mine to run as I saw fit. He wouldn't meddle. I trusted his business sense, and I wasn't worried about it being successful. Ironically, I had thought about studying hotel manage-ment in college, but had decided to get a more general business degree, and now 10 years later I was considering starting a hotel business.

Later that day on my way back to the East Coast, I sat on the plane contemplating the weekend events and the difference they would make in my life. I loved being on the East Coast and had mixed feelings about moving west so soon, but I was confident opening a hotel was the perfect business opportunity for me. I knew it was time for me to make this next life-changing step.

Now in my late twenties, I decided it was about time to focus on one romantic relationship at a time. I had spent a lot of time testing the waters, and I knew I needed to start seriously dating.

I had a boyfriend in Chicago at the time I met Chuck, yet I couldn't help but feel a pull toward Chuck. I enjoyed our chance meeting in Calgary and remembered how much fun we had together. Even though I was not sure either guy was "Mr. Right," I felt reluctant to break off my Chicago romance that I had recently committed to. Had I really given that guy a shot? Was I ever going to be able to be committed to anyone long term or had I gotten so used to the dating game that I couldn't give it up for one person? Not to mention that neither guy lived anywhere near Utah. I needed to make a choice.

I went back to Connecticut knowing that my time there was running out—I would be moving to Utah to launch the hotel within six months. As soon as I arrived home, I heard from Chuck. He wanted to see me again. I told him no, explaining that I wouldn't be in Connecticut for much longer and that I had a boyfriend in Chicago. But Chuck was persistent. He put the hard sell on me. He sent me flowers, and even faxed me his résumé! He was courting me in a big way. And to top it off, he was incredibly sweet. We clicked during every brief interaction we had, even if it was a simple phone call. I decided to meet him for dinner in New York City. Just like Calgary, we had a blast together. It was so comfortable. During the next few weeks I reemphasized to Chuck that we were just friends. But by Thanksgiving, I knew that we were more than friends. I was falling in love.

By Christmas, I had made up my mind. I didn't want to be just friends with Chuck any longer. I wanted more. I knew that Chuck's patience was running out and that I was close to losing him. My official boyfriend at the time, the one from Chicago, was in town for the holidays. Despite the horrible timing, I decided to break our relationship off. From that moment on, I was committed to Chuck.

I spent the next several months preparing to move back to Utah. Chuck and I were seriously dating by then, but in the back of my mind I was worried that our relationship was bound to end. My only hope lay in that he had been trying to move to California when we

Chuck Maggelet and Crystal safely on the ground at Bear Lake after Chuck's first helicopter ride with his future father-in-law, Jay, April 1992.

started dating, so at least he had an interest in being out West. But I also knew that Utah was not California.

Chuck had already purchased his first house in New Hampshire. So it was reassuring to have him by my side, helping me find a house in Utah. His dad had been in the army, so as a child he moved around a lot. Since he hadn't been to Utah since he was a child, he was excited to visit there again.

It was during one of those weekends that Chuck asked me, "Why are you looking for such a tiny house?" I was honest with him. I didn't see the point in owning a large home when only I would be living there. I had never owned a house and I wanted to start out small. I also didn't want to deter would-be boyfriends by intimidating them with a large house. Chuck did not seem too fazed by my statement and continued to look at real estate with me, always encouraging me to look at bigger homes.

Even though Chuck accompanied me a number of times on my Utah house hunting, it wasn't until April 1993 that I invited my dad to meet Chuck. We drove from the airport straight to Dad's home in

Brigham City. Chuck was surprised to see more than just a cabin. It wasn't the sight of horses or even the llamas; what hit him as unusual was finding my dad sitting in a helicopter.

"Good to finally meet you, Chuck. Would you like to go for a ride?" my dad asked.

Chuck accepted the offer, and once we left the ground he asked my dad, "So how long have you been flying?"

Without missing a beat my dad answered, "Counting today?" At that moment I knew all would be well between my two favorite men.

By the time we purchased our first home, Chuck had proposed and we were to be married. We moved to Utah together, and finding the right partner was never an issue again. I'm glad I took the time to get to know myself before committing to a life partner. I had learned what I wanted in a partner as well as what I could offer someone else, and this union with Chuck was an answer to all the right questions. We were married in October, just one year after our weekend in Calgary.

Crystal and Chuck on their wedding day, October 23, 1993.

Partners in Marriage and Business

Principle: Take opportunities in life when they present themselves.

I wasn't nervous about starting the hotel in Salt Lake. I truly believe that if you are given an opportunity that interests you, you just figure it out. You might not do everything right and you might mess up along the way, but you figure it out.

My dad first sent me to Oregon, where I spent a month with a friend and business partner who had developed a hotel concept that my dad felt would work for us in Salt Lake. It was a crash course in hotel construction and management, from working at the front desk and housekeeping to meeting with potential contractors. With just a few weeks of focused training, I hit the ground running—or stumbling—but I was on my way. It was nonstop work during that first year. I was in charge of the hotel from the ground up, liter-ally. There were still six existing buildings standing on the land we had acquired, so my first steps were to find a demolition company to tear them down and to finalize a name. Early on, my dad had proposed the name Crystal Suites, but I didn't really want the hotels to bear my name. I hired a brand designer to come up with logos and names. He came back with several options, but nothing seemed right. In the end, I grew to love the Crystal Inn name and logo. It was simple, attractive, and memorable.

As I worked to construct and open a hotel and plan a wedding, I had little time to become too caught up in the many rumors that were floating around the Salt Lake lodging community. I was perceived as Jay Call's daughter, who had been given a hotel as a wedding gift. The girl with no hotel experience. I knew that some people were leery that I could be successful, but their doubts only motivated me more. Despite what industry peers believed, my dad did not buy me a hotel for a wedding gift. Aside from identifying the best location, everything else was Chuck's and my blood, sweat, and tears. Moreover, the hotel management company and ownership of our hotel wasn't going to be a part of Flying J at all.

As I continued on my quest to build the first hotel, I didn't always have the right answers or know what to do, but I was lucky to be surrounded by a strong support network. First and foremost, my dad was happy to answer questions or direct me to others who could. Also, in the beginning I was able to work with Flying J's in-house real estate, legal, and finance executives, which was a great advantage for a first-time entrepreneur. I wasn't shy about asking for advice—looking dumb never scared me. I knew that it was much worse to pretend you understood something when you really didn't get it. Needless to say, I counted on many Flying J employees to advise me in those early days, and I greatly appreciated their help.

Building the Salt Lake City hotel wasn't an easy process. Once the land was ready, I met with contractors, secured financing, managed marketing—everything was on my shoulders. Each decision that first year came down to me. It was challenging to know exactly what to do and when to do it, but it was also a profound learning experience. I recognized early on that I had to make decisions, that I couldn't be passive or indecisive. I had always embraced hard work, but this was a whole new level of details and people to manage. It was up to me to keep moving the project forward at record speed, because we had a tight deadline. We had signed a contract to rent all our rooms to guests just six months after we broke ground. Making this commitment added to the stress level, but also ensured the hotel would open with a bang. It was challenging, but I believed the payoff would be worth it.

Chuck was my number one day-to-day advisor and confidant. Though he was working with AT&T at the time, he always took whatever time I needed to offer help or a listening ear. He wanted to see the hotel succeed, and his analytical skills complemented my marketing skills. He put building the Salt Lake hotel first before anything else in our newlywed life. He never complained about the work it entailed. We were barely able to take a honeymoon and all of our playful dating days were long over.

Like me, Chuck knew that starting a new company required sacrifice, and we hoped and believed eventually those sacrifices would pay off. It all was a bit overwhelming, but it was also incredibly exciting. I began by organizing everything there was to do on color-coded index cards, with over 100 individual cards and tasks. Those index cards, organized by the categories "construction," "marketing," and "operations," kept me on task and wearing the right hat at the right time, and I religiously stayed on schedule.

The biggest lesson I learned during that whirlwind of a year was to believe in myself. I had to make decisions on the fly—there was no other choice. I gained more confidence by working hard and overcoming challenges—challenges that many people in the industry didn't think I could overcome. Here I was starting a business in an industry I knew nothing about. I had never worked in the hospitality field before, and some wondered, "What could she possibly know?" I did not have any time to worry about what others thought. It was counterproductive to getting the job done and showing the naysayers I could do it.

Preparing for Our First Guests

My dad's vision for Crystal Inn couldn't have been more spot on. Salt Lake had a booming tourist industry. More and more, the state was becoming known as a great destination for tourists and conventions, and the city needed more hotel rooms to accommodate the growth. The Salt Lake Convention & Visitors Bureau was always supportive of the hotel. The minute we broke ground on the Salt Lake site, I was already booking rooms.

Crystal and Chuck at the first Crystal Inn in Salt Lake City in 1994.

I wasn't intimidated. I may have been naïve, but I believed I could get the hotel built and open on time, and I worked toward that goal never doubting it would happen. I knew it was an awesome opportunity, and I wasn't going to let it pass me by. It was clear from the beginning there was a market need for the Salt Lake hotel. The market demand and our commitment to have the hotel open by a certain date kept me motivated to push harder and harder. What became challenging was the time frame we were working under. City officials and the Salt Lake Convention & Visitors Bureau were pushing me to rent rooms as soon as possible.

The first guests I booked were a group of women bowlers traveling to Salt Lake City to compete in a bowling competition in early April 1994. I was so excited to have guests on the docket, but I also knew I now had an inflexible schedule. Their upcoming stay meant I had a hard deadline to meet.

We weren't ready to open by the time their stay approached, and I was starting to panic. I didn't want to open until everything was perfect. But they were coming and I couldn't say, "Would you mind delaying your tournament for another week or two?" Hotels throughout the city were full, so there was no alternative place to move them. I wondered what I was thinking when I booked them months ago. I thought I had given myself plenty of buffer time, but I didn't understand how construction could easily be delayed.

We were moving furniture into the hotel over Easter weekend. Everyone had been working hard, so I decided to give our employees a break to enjoy the holiday. But we still needed to get the furniture moved in and set up before the bowlers arrived on April 6.

A family dropped by on April 2, the Saturday morning before Easter. A bride was interested in booking rooms for her wedding guests. We weren't even close to being ready for the bowlers, let alone ready to show a bride how perfect our rooms would be for her guests. She seemed to be on a budget and I saw an opportunity, so I offered her a deal: "If you come back to the hotel tomorrow and bring everyone you know to help us finish moving furniture in, I'll let you have the honeymoon suite free of charge."

The next day our hotel was filled with the bride's friends and family, helping us move furniture and adding the final touches before our grand opening. We couldn't have done it without them. We made our deadline, the bowling team had a place to stay, and the newlyweds enjoyed the complimentary room.

Just as the first hotel was opening in April 1994, my dad and Chuck went for a drive along the Wasatch Front. Unbeknownst to me, my dad was about to convince Chuck to leave AT&T. But it didn't take much convincing—Chuck also saw enormous potential in the Crystal Inn concept and brand we were creating and was already weighing the idea of joining our efforts. Chuck was excited to work with Crystal Inn. He believed in the concept and was willing to pay back his monetary commitment to AT&T, which had paid for his Harvard education, to start officially with Crystal Inn in the summer of 1994.

I was ecstatic when Chuck agreed with my dad and joined the Crystal Inn team. I had secretly hoped we would work together. Now united, we hatched a plan to build a chain of hotels near business hubs, and to possibly team with Flying J to build hotels at several of their travel plazas. It was nice knowing that our goals would be aligned at home and at work. It seemed like a dream come true— just like how my parents had started Flying J together so many years before. I realized that it wouldn't always be easy, but for the most part things always worked out. As the hotel business grew, my relationship with Chuck grew stronger. Marrying Chuck turned out to be the best decision I ever made. He supported me more than I ever could have imagined. We were partners. We were building something great—and we were building it together.

Chuck became the chief site selector. He traveled the country searching for the best possible locations for new hotels. While Chuck was on the hunt for new hotel sites, I maintained the role of opening each new hotel. Chuck and I worked in tandem. We balanced each other out. On the home front and at the office we talked about work nonstop. We were learning more in our newlywed years about each other and how to work together than most longtime couples *ever* find out about each other. In the beginning it was very difficult, especially given the innocent bliss we had experienced during our courtship. Our relationship had been based on being playmates, not work colleagues. Our approaches at work were very different. Chuck is very analytical and I am more a gut-feeling person, which caused for many heated discussions. But luckily we valued having a successful marriage far above anything else, so we worked through our differences, often coming to a better answer together.

Before we officially opened the Salt Lake hotel, we broke ground on our second location in Brigham City, Utah. My confidence was at a record high. I knew I could do this. After a year of nonstop work and stress, I could finally see the pieces coming together. My dad saw it too. We were convinced the hotels would take off, and after building two hotels and seeing their success we wanted to create a company to build a hotel chain.

In July 1994, Chuck and I launched our new company. By combining our surname of Maggelet with my maiden name of Call, we decided on the company name of MacCall Management, LLC. We officially had a hotel management and development company focused on building a chain of hotels.

Our first two hotels were on their way and we were searching for the next opportunity. A natural fit, or so we thought, was taking over the management of Flying J's seven motel properties. We decided to approach Phil Adams about our idea.

"Flying J isn't focused on hotels, and we can help to build out a hotel chain at travel plazas where it makes sense," I said to Phil. "Let us take over the motels. We are building a management team and a management company focused on lodging."

My dad and Phil agreed. Flying J had plenty of distractions already. In many ways, it made sense for us to take over the Flying J hotels. Building and managing hotels was our primary priority, and a distraction for Flying J.

Nearly overnight, Chuck and I went from managing two hotels to nine. We were ramping up what was already a crazy schedule and fast-growth mode. It was hard and exhausting, but we were motivated and determined.

As with any takeover, we were confronted with several challenges. We suddenly had hundreds of employees. We needed to build and sustain a positive culture, as well as start offering benefits like health insurance. We needed to develop a business plan that would ensure we were scaling the business sustainably. It was truly a baptism by fire, and we were inexperienced. The only thing that kept us going was our confidence and determination. We didn't have all the answers, but we knew we could find them. We kept at it, working night and day to figure things out. By January 1995, we had taken over all seven Flying J hotel properties.

Growth was a significant challenge. There were so many opportunities and so much work to do we couldn't build a staff fast enough to manage it all. We had a general manager and an accounting system in place, but we needed to hire some home office staff. We could only hire an accountant and payroll manager, which were critical positions, and found ourselves relying on people to do much more than they were capable of, which didn't always end well. But there were also people who rose to the occasion and became some of our best staff members.

The early days of Crystal Inn had ups and downs like any business.

Chuck and I learned several lessons during the first years. We spent way too much time working and talking about work. Our colleagues became our only friends, which worked great until suddenly they stopped performing at work. It also meant that Chuck and I spent too much time debating business issues or addressing business needs to spend time on our relationship. For better or worse, our world revolved around the business.

Despite the commotion we experienced those first few years, Chuck and I were ecstatic at the opportunity to be at the helm of what was becoming a successful small independent hotel chain. For the most part my dad stayed out of our way. He only offered advice when we sought it, or when he saw an opportunity that he didn't want us to miss. For example, my dad thought we should build in Logan, Utah. He thought Logan was an up-and-coming destination. Chuck researched the location and gave the project the green light. We decided to go with it. And my dad was right—Logan was wildly successful.

In the summer of 1995, my dad and Phil approached us with another opportunity they thought would enhance both the Crystal Inn hotel chain and Flying J. They wanted us to consider building hotels near Flying J travel plazas. They were convinced the hotels would be successful, and we saw potential in their plan. Because of the sheer number of Flying J plazas, most of which had access to land ideally sized for a hotel site, we recognized the potential to build and spread across the country. We knew it could be challenging but thought there was great growth potential since Flying J already owned so much property.

Flying J executives compiled a list of the top 20 plaza sites that they thought would complement our hotel concept. As we looked at their plan, we recognized early on that it might not work. The Flying J concept was substantially different than the brand we had established for Crystal Inn. Chuck and I began to fear that the two brands were far too different to work in sync. But we weren't ready to close our minds to the idea, because we still saw enormous potential if the factors could line up. We were, however, beginning to doubt whether everything would fall into place as we had once hoped.

Despite our skepticism, we decided to explore our options further. If we determined that the concept made sense, our hope was to start breaking ground at these sites as soon as possible. Chuck began flying across the country, examining each travel plaza and potential location. We knew the Crystal Inn concept and who our primary customers were, so Chuck's goal was to make sure the Crystal Inn concept would easily complement Flying J plazas. Every little detail counted, from location off the freeway to clientele base. I trusted that Chuck wouldn't green-light a project unless he was confident that we were making the right move. I anxiously awaited Chuck's approval. If it worked, the growth potential of our hotel chain would be enormous. But when Chuck arrived home he was deflated. Without sugarcoating the news, Chuck told me flat out, "There's maybe one or two plazas that might work with our concept but that's all."

My dad and Phil remained convinced the hotels would be successful, but Chuck and I were skeptical. Against our better judgment, Chuck and I decided to pick the very best of the sites and try opening hotels. We built new Crystal Inns at three of four potential Flying J locations. We broke ground in Gulfport, Mississippi, in the fall of 1995, and the hotel was open for business by the beginning of the next year. Just as we feared, the Gulfport hotel was a dud. It didn't take us into the red, but the return on our investment was nowhere near that of the other hotels we had built. The primary problem was the hotel's location. It was situated one freeway exit away from where all the major restaurants and shopping options were, which meant it was one exit away from where all the lodging traffic wanted to be. The next two hotels built on Flying J property didn't enjoy our typical average daily rate. The freeway clientele were tough, and they were rougher on the rooms and harder on the staff. The freeway locations were also more seasonal, which didn't give as good a return.

Unfortunately these three new hotels were never as successful as the locations Chuck and I picked ourselves that were not by Flying J travel plazas. We quickly learned that location matters. We were better off acquiring more ideally located sites, not cheaper sites, and attracting patrons that were interested in suburban locations closer to the activities of the city.

Over time there were two lessons that came from the Gulfport property. First, it solidified what Chuck and I already knew: our concept and brand were unique from Flying J's. We had developed a model that was working. Second, with limited capital we needed to shift plans and make sure we only built in the very best places we could find for our concept.

We told Phil what the Gulfport hotel was experiencing—that it wasn't working like he and my dad had envisioned. If they wanted to explore building hotels near their travel plazas, they needed to work with another hotel management company. The Crystal Inn concept wasn't what they needed. It wasn't right for their clientele.

Phil and my dad understood, and we stopped building adjacent to Flying J plazas. Other hotel management companies proposed business plans to work with them, and we reviewed them and helped determine whether they were viable. But none of the other plans ever came to fruition. No one ever came up with the dollars and plans to make it happen.

It was difficult saying no to building hotels across the country, which would have meant fast growth for our relatively young company. But by that point we had proven our independence from Flying J. We wanted to make decisions that were right for our growing business. Yet I still sought my father's approval. I wanted him to be proud of me. Saying no was hard for me to do, but it was the right decision.

Saying no to building alongside Flying J plazas took a weight off my shoulders, since now we could focus on one strategy to build near business hubs. We began scouting new sites that were closer to home. Our next hotels were built in West Valley and Midvale, Utah.

The sites to build on were chosen to fit our model of being adjacent to businesses, restaurants, and activities, while also being priced for the cost-conscious traveler. Our plan was working. We coined our mission statement: "Delight every guest everyday one at a time." We wanted to be the budget-conscious travelers' home away from home.

In the late 1990s, my dad suggested we build in Great Falls, Montana. We trusted his instinct and decided to go for it. But by that time, we were beginning to worry that too many markets were being inundated with new hotel properties. We decided to cease building new properties and focus on managing our already-established hotels, as well as acquire existing hotel sites and renovate them to fit the Crystal Inn brand. The Great Falls location was the last hotel we built from the ground up.

Our next hotels were in St. George and Cedar City, Utah. We saw enormous opportunity in these emerging markets to rebrand already-existing properties. These were the first two hotels we didn't build from scratch. This presented a new challenge, because we had to decide whether we should put the Crystal Inn brand on a hotel that wasn't ours. Neither of the properties came close to fitting our cookie-cutter model—a model we had finally perfected. We played with different branding, names, and colors. In the end I decided that our brand was really about cleanliness and good service—not about the layout of the hotel. As long as the hotel met those basic criteria, I'd be happy to put the Crystal Inn name on it.

We renovated the St. George and Cedar City hotels to match our concept, and they filled our holes in the Utah market. By 2002 we were managing 14 hotel properties.

Entering a New Stage—Motherhood

Not long after I was married and in the middle of starting MacCall Management, I began to hear my biological clock ticking. I knew I needed to get on this children thing if I were ever going to have a family. It was far from the ideal time to start having children, but I didn't want to wait any longer. Chuck and I knew starting a family was our next challenge—and we were ready.

In just 24 months, I went from being a single, working woman living a cushy life on the East Coast to becoming a married entrepreneur building a hotel business in Utah and about to start a family. It was about as drastic a change as one can experience, and I loved it. My dad thought I was crazy. He was worried I was moving too fast—that I was living too much of life in a few short years. But I felt differently. I loved how busy and productive I was. My dream had come true. I was starting a business and a family with the man of my dreams.

Just two weeks before my first baby was due, I was scheduled to attend our annual conference for the managers of our hotel properties on September 5 and 6, 1995. The conference was a much-anticipated event for our organization, and I had to be there. I wasn't worried about attending. I knew I could handle it. But just when you think you're ready, life throws you a curveball.

On September 1, I gave birth to our first child, Drew. He came nearly three weeks early, and I had to have a cesarean, but I still made the managers' conference less than a week later. There is no maternity leave for entrepreneurs, so I was now doing the seemingly impossible task of juggling new motherhood with entrepreneurship. When I look back, I don't know how I got through those first few weeks and months, but I managed and was happy.

I knew that bringing a child into the world would change my life, but I had a luxury that most women don't—I was in complete

Crystal's young son, Drew, entertaining himself in the Logan Crystal Inn lobby.

control of my home and work situation. I could bring Drew to the office, to meetings, and on business trips with me. I was my own boss and could manage childcare in the office. I didn't think twice about bringing Drew wherever I needed to be. I have vivid memories of nursing him under a blanket as I walked the construction site of our latest new hotel. Most meetings were filled with men who were used to their wives—and of course children—staying at home during the day. I didn't let the odd looks faze me. This was a family company and I wasn't going to let anyone or anything—including my own insecurities—stop me from reaching my goals of owning a successful business *and* being a successful mother.

Life at home and at the office got a little trickier when I gave birth to my first daughter, Lexi, in 1997. Having two young children required more help and organization, but we still managed to make it work. I was so happy to have a healthy boy and girl. They were the perfect distraction for Chuck and me to leave business behind and focus on our young family.

Chuck and I talked for hours on end about whether we wanted to bring a third child into our family. We both immensely enjoyed our two children. The heartfelt joy we experienced watching our little children grow was unmatched, and we realized we wanted to have additional kids more than we wanted to grow the company at the same pace we had been. In addition, we believed many markets were getting overbuilt with lodging properties and decided it would not be a bad idea to slow down our hotel growth. We decided to try for a third child. As we started planning, we recognized and agreed that I would have to slow down at work or at home. In my heart, I knew that I couldn't give 100 percent to a third child and to my work at the hotels. I couldn't be everything to everyone. Chuck agreed with the predicament we were in. Together we decided it was time for my role at the office to diminish—at least temporarily. I knew I would have the luxury of participating in the big decisions, so I was not too concerned about leaving the day-to-day management to Chuck and our staff.

I was ecstatic when I learned I was pregnant with our third child. I went in for a routine checkup and my doctor mentioned that a study of expectant mothers was taking place at the University of Utah, including a free ultrasound at 12 weeks. Even as a mother carrying her third child, you never pass up the chance for a free ultrasound. Chuck wanted to stay back—there was so much work to do and it was just an ultrasound; he'd been through that drill with the other two kids.

"There's always work to do," I told him. "This is the first ultrasound and I want you there."

We sat in the office, waiting to see the first images of our baby, but all we could see was a blurry image. We had done this before and weren't quite sure why the image looked so blurry.

"Were you on fertility drugs?" the nurse asked us.

"No," Chuck and I responded in sync.

"Well, there are two in there," she responded. "Looks like you conceived twins the old-fashioned way."

"Two?" I asked.

She nodded yes with a smile. Chuck and I were having twins. At that moment I knew my life as I knew it was over. The thought took a while to settle in my head. I was in shock now; after a tough decision to have three kids, we would be having *four*. I should never have joked about not wanting an odd number of kids or wanting twins.

In 2000, Erica and Hailey were born. We now had four kids five years old and under. My perfect plan had not worked out so well, but they were healthy, and I was grateful to have them.

Just as we had planned, I cut back working at the office for the next several years. My attention turned to my four young children. In just a few short years my life had flipped completely. From being a robust career woman and entrepreneur, I became a mother with four children to care for. I was dedicated to my children and caring for them. I loved being a mom. Yet I couldn't stop the nagging feeling that I was missing out on something. I still had a small role in the hotels and remained on the Flying J Board of Directors, but I spent hardly any time at the office. I attended Flying J board and management meetings at the corporate office in nearby Ogden, but that was it. I felt out of the loop. I knew to the outside world I seemed to have it all—a beautiful, healthy family and a thriving business. I could work when I wanted *and* I could be a full-time mom. Even though these were very happy years, I did not feel content. I wasn't good at playing dolls or cars. I found I spent much more time *organizing* my kids' lives than playing with them. I remembered that even as a child I really did not like to play, so maybe this is why it was hard as a mother. Logically I knew I was making the best decision for my children, but I couldn't help wondering if it was the right decision for me.

At the time, I didn't recognize how unfulfilled I had become. I was playing the role of perfect mom. I was well on my way to becoming the best helicopter mom, because I had so much energy and it was largely directed at my kids' lives. I would look at my beautiful family and was so grateful. We were truly happy and had so much. Everything was as it should have been. I had dinner on the table every night. We had memorable traditions, fun vacations, and beautiful holidays. Our kids were in every activity available to them. Meanwhile, everything was running smoothly at Crystal Inn and MacCall Management. I reviewed the financial statements and all was well. The business was successful. Our family was happy. Chuck was happy.

Why wasn't I content? It's a strange feeling, being happy and empty at the same time, but that's how I felt.

Before I knew it, my life was turning into a traditional "mom" life. I didn't want to be a stereotypical stay-at-home mom. I felt a longing to be working, but I didn't want to put my career before my children. There was a dichotomous force pulling me in both directions. It was tough. Like so many other women, it was hard to balance desire for a meaningful career and desire to be there to

At an elephant refuge in Africa with (front to back) Erica, Hailey, Lexi, Drew, and Chuck Maggelet, March 2006.

care for family. Every person has to make hard choices about family and career. Together, Chuck and I decided that I would stay home. I wanted to be home for my children, but I didn't necessarily want that life for myself. In addition, I was not sure it was the example I wanted my children to see.

A Devastating Blow

Principle: Never take great times for granted; life can change quickly in very unexpected ways.

On March 15, 2003, I received a phone call—the kind of call everyone fears. The kind of call you worry about getting one day, but never really think will happen. It had been a busy weekend. It was the weekend before St. Patrick's Day. I had run the Leprechaun Lope 5K in the morning, and in the evening we took the kids to *Disney on Ice*. Just as the show was ending, my cell phone rang; one of my dad's closest friends was on the other end.

"Crystal?" he said anxiously.

"Yes, this is Crystal."

"Hi, Crystal. I'm here with Tamra at your dad's house. We don't know where your dad is."

"What do you mean you don't know where he is? He's missing?"

He went on to tell me that my dad had been flying his good friend and former vice president of refining, Buzz Germer, and his wife, Ilene, to their home in Sun Valley, Idaho. Buzz had been undergoing cancer treatment at the Huntsman Cancer Hospital at the University of Utah. He had just been released to go home. He was still quite ill and Jay wanted to fly them to get them home quickly. For Jay, it should have been a quick, easy flight on a Saturday afternoon. His flight plan had them scheduled to land in Sun Valley around 2 p.m. Their plane lost contact with air traffic control at 1:45 p.m.

It was a blustery March day in Salt Lake. It had been cold, wet, and gray all weekend, and a storm was moving in that evening. I was told that a search crew had been called to look for my dad's plane, but weather forced them to call off the search after just an hour. My heart wanted to believe that my dad was fine. He was an experienced pilot, with 20,000 hours of flight time logged. Maybe he had trouble and had landed somewhere, I thought to myself. My gut instinct spoke differently. I feared for my dad. I feared for Tamra, my dad's wife. I feared for Buzz and Ilene. Chuck, Tamra, and I sped away to Hailey, Idaho, where the search was headquartered. Though we made the 280-mile drive to Hailey in record time, it was the longest drive of my life. We didn't know what to expect.

Had he landed somewhere?

Was he hurt?

Was he gone?

We arrived at the Blaine County Sheriff's Office a few hours before dawn.

"Get some rest," they told us. "We'll start searching the moment the sun rises."

Their assurances didn't ease our fears. We were helpless.

Later that morning, Tamra, Chuck, and I sat in the back of a small conference room, listening intensely as the search crew planned their next steps. We hung on every word they said, searching for a hint of hope. We knew the weather had been bad. We knew the plane lost contact 15 minutes before it was scheduled to land. Still, we were hopeful. Dad was a phenomenal pilot and had routinely flown dangerous search and rescue missions looking for lost hikers in mountainous locations.

Out of nowhere—or so it seemed—we heard a searcher say, "The last thing we know is the plane was headed into the ground at 300 miles an hour."

As he finished the sentence, Tamra let out a horrific scream, unlike anything I had ever heard before. The deputy's statement instantaneously blew a hole through the three of us. We hadn't heard anything like what he had said until that moment. At that point, we knew there were no doubts about my dad, Buzz, and Ilene. They hadn't landed somewhere else. They weren't lost. They weren't merely hurt. Their plane had crashed into the ground going 300 miles per hour!

They were gone.

We never should have been in the briefing room. The search crew tried to comfort Tamra as she sobbed, but she was inconsolable. They assured us that nothing was final until the wreckage was found. But we knew. Chuck and I finally calmed Tamra down and together we walked lifelessly out of the room.

Chuck and I returned and continued to listen. Within minutes dispatch called in.

"We think we've found the wreckage," we heard a voice say. Everything was surreal. We were living a nightmare. The radio continued streaming.

"I think this is a wallet."

"Here's a piece of the tail."

"I don't think there are any survivors."

I was in complete shock. In the back of your mind, everyone knows tragedy can strike at any time. Yet here I was, completely blown away. My dad was gone. Buzz and Ilene were gone. A deputy walked Chuck and me out of the room. Tamra knew my dad's tragic fate the moment she saw us. There was nothing to say. Our hearts were broken.

We returned to Salt Lake City and went through the motions. We made an announcement to the company employees, to the press, and began planning my dad's services. Losing my dad was one of the most traumatic experiences that I've ever faced. I had never lost anyone nearly that close to me before. I tried to stay positive after my dad's death. After my parents' divorce, my dad and I were never as close as I wanted to be. Yet after his death I felt grateful for the distance that had grown between us. I know his death would have been far more difficult if we had been closer. We didn't spend much time together outside of the workplace. We would get together at Christmas for dinner and maybe a weekend at his ranch in Montana once a year, but he was not a part of my day-to-day life. There were few family traditions or holiday memories to mourn. Mostly I missed knowing he'd be there if I needed him for fatherly advice. Luckily for me, just a few months before he had explicitly told me how proud he was of me.

I took a long time to process what our family had just been through. I worried immensely for Tamra. I couldn't imagine losing Chuck; I really had no idea the pain she must have felt. For years, Tamra and my dad had been each other's everything. He was her life. I knew Tamra would face the most pain from our loss. Though she would be financially secure, she would be forced to build a completely new life. Besides Tamra, Jay left behind his two children, Thad and me, six grandchildren, his mother, and four siblings.

My dad's tragic death left a void in our family and in Flying J. Though my dad was not playing a day-to-day role in the company at the time of his passing, he was vital to keeping the company moving steadily forward and ensuring that the company's growth, though aggressive, was also responsible. At the time of his death he was playing more of a watchful consulting role within the company, which at the time employed 11,000 workers and had annual sales of $4.6 billion. He'd entrusted the appointed executive team to keep the company growing, and he rarely stepped in to counter the direction they were taking. Just a few months before his death, I remember my dad telling me how fulfilling his life had been, and how he had never dreamed Flying J would grow to the size and have the success it had. The month he died in March 2003, Flying J had a record-breaking net income of $30 million.

In his role as CEO and president, Phil Adams oversaw Flying J's short- and long-term strategies that were critical to the company's fast-paced growth. There was no question that Phil would continue his leadership role upon my dad's passing. But serving as CEO and president without my dad's watchful eye gave Phil nearly complete control of Flying J.

Flying J experienced some of its most astounding growth during the 2000s. The company was predominantly a downstream marketer, with a heavy concentration on its retail assets, which were profitable. The company's refineries were also quite profitable, as were its exploration and production assets, though finding oil and gas reserves wasn't the company's top priority. Under Phil's leadership, Flying J's focus was centered on customer relationships. Phil wanted to own the customer experience and relationship, and he launched several initiatives that put the company on that path.

Phil wanted Flying J to eventually control freight movement across North America. He viewed freight movement and management as an enormous opportunity for Flying J. He believed that the right hauler should move the right load at the right time, and that Flying J could make it happen. It was a monumental part of his grand vision for Flying J's future.

Many industry leaders didn't recognize Phil's vision. Nor did they see how the steps he took—some riskier than others—were attempts to accomplish his goals. Instead, many thought he was an overly ambitious executive. Jay always trusted Phil's business instincts and acumen. He knew Phil was a phenomenal visionary and powerful leader who could get things done. Moreover, he was a risk-taker who saw opportunities when others shied away. Phil had taken Flying J to places that Jay had never envisioned.

I also trusted Phil. Under his leadership, Flying J had skyrocketing revenues and robust operations. Though we didn't always see eye to eye—which I believe can be healthy—I thought Phil was the right executive to move the company forward. However, two of the acquisitions Phil made during his tenure made me nervous: the Longhorn Pipeline and the Bakersfield Refinery.

The Promise and Pitfalls of the Longhorn Pipeline

For years the Southwest region had struggled to get the fuel its growing population demanded. Arizona, which lacked its own locally based refinery, consumed millions of gallons of fuel from California each day. The Longhorn Pipeline was anticipated to be a profitable solution to ease the Southwest's predicted fuel crunch. Originally built in the 1950s by Exxon Corporation, the Longhorn Pipeline extended from the Texas Gulf Coast across the Lone Star State to its terminus in El Paso. Though the pipeline promised to carry much-needed fuel across Texas and into the Southwest region, Longhorn failed to overcome economic and political hurdles and sat unused for decades until it was acquired by Dallas-based Longhorn Pipeline Partners, which was owned by a group of companies that included ExxonMobil and BP Amoco.

Recognizing the Southwest's increasing need for fuel, Longhorn Pipeline Partners was determined to revamp the aged and outdated pipeline. The organization released an ambitious plan to invest $300 million to lay 250 miles of pipe and modernize the entire Longhorn Pipeline infrastructure. Its goal was to transport gasoline, diesel, and jet fuel from Gulf Coast refiners to Odessa and El Paso. From El Paso, the pipeline was to connect to a robust grid of branching pipelines that would pump nearly 10 million gallons of fuel each day into Arizona and New Mexico. Beyond supplying much-needed fuel to the Southwest region, Longhorn promised to relieve California's petroleum industry, which was being drained by the region's growing fuel consumption and demand. It was an ambitious and highly anticipated project, and it was a project that faced mounting hurdles.

From nearly the moment Longhorn Pipeline Partners announced its ambitious plan, the project was hindered by a multitude of operational, political, and financial challenges. Progress was slow, with nearly no major milestones accomplished during its first few years.

In 1998, the project faced turmoil as it was confronted with lawsuits from competitors and environmental advocates, including Hill Country ranchers, the City of Austin, and the Lower Colorado River Authority. A judge issued an injunction, and the project came to a screeching halt. Longhorn's opponents questioned the 50-year-old pipeline's structural integrity and argued it posed an environmental threat to nearby communities. Years passed while the pipeline sat unutilized and aging as the U.S. Environmental Protection Agency and the U.S. Department of Transportation reviewed the case.

Legal issues finally subsided in 2001 and construction to upgrade the aging pipeline resumed. But by the end of 2002, the project lost financial support and the pipeline again sat idle while Longhorn Pipeline Partners scrambled to recapitalize the once highly anticipated project. It wasn't until 2004 that construction was back on track and the partially renovated pipeline began moving fuel 700 miles across Texas. Though fuel was finally flowing through the pipeline, the project hit yet another snag when it failed to reach branching pipelines and deliver the fuel to Arizona, where demand was at an all-time high.

Under Phil's direction, Flying J stepped dramatically into the Longhorn story in 2006. Though the Longhorn Pipeline had faced years of ups and downs—mostly downs—Phil believed in its promise to relieve the growing fuel demand of the Southwest and was convinced it could scale up capacity to meet forthcoming demand more cheaply than West Texas or California refiners could. Moreover, he believed Longhorn was an immense opportunity that had potential to continue Flying J's growth, if the right management team took over its operations.

In the spring of 2006, Flying J approached Longhorn Pipeline Partners about acquiring the troubled operation. The group was ready to rid themselves of the project and agreed to the acquisition. By August, Flying J had acquired 100 percent ownership. Though Phil and Flying J executives were ecstatic, the acquisition bemused industry insiders, who thought the risk wasn't worth taking, especially since Flying J had just consummated the purchase of the plagued Bakersfield Refinery. But Flying J had a well-earned reputation of being the industry's risk-taker, and one that more often than not came out on top. Still, many wondered whether the pipeline even offered value to the market, or if so, if Flying J was biting off more than it could chew.

Phil and the executive team believed wholeheartedly in the Longhorn Pipeline. They believed without a doubt that Longhorn could deliver product into the Phoenix and Tucson areas significantly cheaper than California product could travel from west to east.

The Flying J executive team also believed that Longhorn would be the dominant player in the region, competing with Western Refining in El Paso and Navajo Refining in Artesia, New Mexico. Longhorn, the team believed, was a far superior asset, which would ultimately create a significant competitive advantage in the Southwest region. Flying J execs always believed that with the superior asset the company would come out on top in the long term. But Longhorn Pipeline was far from profitable at the time of its acquisition by Flying J. Since its inception the pipeline had faced hurdle after hurdle and was never able to deliver on its promises. And as Flying J would soon discover, more challenges were ahead.

Flying J approached Shell about a possible partnership. Shell's Port Arthur Refinery was already planning an expansion—an expansion Flying J execs thought would complement the Longhorn Pipeline. Flying J believed Shell's refinery would be able to connect to the Longhorn Pipeline and become the pipeline's primary fuel supply source. It expected Shell would recognize the partnership opportunity, expand its refinery sufficiently, and begin supplying its fuel product, which would eventually flow to Arizona.

In addition to partnering with Shell, Flying J expected that its current partner in India—Reliance Industries—would also become one of the pipeline's primary suppliers when market conditions favored petroleum exports from India into the United States. Ultimately neither Shell nor Reliance Industries were interested in partnering with Longhorn Pipeline, and even the logistics to make such partnerships possible would have made it impractical in the short term.

Flying J failed to secure partnership interests in the pipeline from other Gulf Coast area refineries, or anywhere else. Flying J was forced to become a spot market buyer and was only able to purchase fuel that was left over after the refiners met their contractual obligations. This proved to be a significant disadvantage for Longhorn, as it was forced to buy fuel at prevailing market rates during a time when Gulf Coast refining margins were particularly strong. Without a vested fuel partner and an easy way to get the fuel into the pipeline, Flying J's Longhorn Pipeline couldn't buy discounted fuel supply that would help it turn a profit.

Longhorn's high fixed operational costs proved to be another key challenge. Regardless of its throughput rate or how well it was operating, the pipeline incurred $4 million to $5 million in fixed expenses every month. (The variable costs of operating the pipeline were very minimal.) Moreover, the pipeline couldn't yield a profit without certain market and political outcomes taking place that were outside of Flying J's control.

With volatility in the market, unstable oil prices, and unsecured partners, Longhorn Pipeline struggled throughout its first years of operation under Flying J's ownership.

Even though Longhorn was not profitable, Phil and his team stuck with their vision and spent millions expanding the pipeline. The pipeline was soon running at full capacity with all types of fuel flowing through it, and it was changing the dynamics of the southwestern market. In fact, the pipeline was *flooding* the southwestern market, which had for decades experienced a fuel crunch.

Despite Longhorn running at full capacity it was still not profitable because the presence of its new-to-market supply corresponded with the lowering of local market prices. The strategy ideally was to sell at the highest price possible and buy at the lowest price possible, but the company was now being forced to buy fuel at high prices and sell too low because of the oversupply. Moreover, it wasn't successful attracting any other organizations to ship fuel in any substantial quantities on the pipeline, thereby sharing the market risk; Flying J was the primary shipper. Phil believed that oversupplying the market would eventually take down or scale back the production of competitors, even if it meant a short-term loss for the company.

When the economy began to slow and oil prices dropped, Longhorn's financial losses expanded and the pipeline situation grew troublesome. Longhorn-associated cash losses due to inappropriate hedges and inventory write-downs were staggering, but the crunch didn't stop there. The credit line funding most of the inventory was directly linked to the price of crude oil, and became smaller as market prices decreased. The need to pay back this shrinking line of credit added to the impact of operating losses. The credit line was settled daily, so payments were needed constantly as the unprecedented fall of crude prices continued. By late 2008, keeping this credit line in compliance consumed much-needed cash. Throughout 2008, creative financing was applied recklessly to avoid running out of cash for the growing Longhorn operation.

Bakersfield Refinery Acquisition

Flying J acquired the Bakersfield Refinery in January 2005. Though acquiring the California-based refinery seemed like an essential piece of the puzzle to make Flying J a truly integrated operation, the refinery proved to be another significant challenge.

The Bakersfield Refinery has a storied history in the California market. It opened as the Mohawk Refinery in 1932, producing 1,500 barrels daily. Decades later it was acquired by Shell Oil, which quickly deemed the refinery unprofitable. Shell planned to close the refinery, stating it was too decrepit and outdated to continue operating. Additionally, Shell argued that the Bakersfield area lacked affordable crude oil to refine. Shell executives said closing the refinery was a simple decision to make; the company couldn't afford to upgrade the refinery's archaic structure when a lack of local crude oil supply would nearly ensure the refinery's unprofitability.

Local politicians and consumer advocates were outraged. They viewed the threatened closure as Shell underhandedly boosting the profits of its other refineries. At the time, the refinery was producing 20,000 barrels of reformulated gasoline each day and 15,000 barrels of diesel a day, which was merely 2 percent of California's much-needed gas supply and 6 percent of its diesel supply. Though a seemingly small amount of the state's daily usage, California's ever-mounting gas and diesel demands meant that the relatively small refinery was a vital producer. The Federal Trade Commission (FTC) heard complaints and responded to the outrage by launching an investigation into Shell's refinery closure plans. Before the FTC released a decision, Shell bowed to the pressure and agreed to search for a potential buyer.

Despite its growing troubles, the Flying J executive team saw the Bakersfield Refinery as an opportunity to enter California's fuel market. Though Flying J had grown to become the country's largest truck plaza operator, it had less experience refining fuel. Since the 1980s, the company had operated small refineries in Cheyenne, Wyoming, and North Salt Lake, Utah, but nothing the magnitude of Bakersfield.

In January 2005, Flying J entered into an agreement with Shell to acquire the refinery for $130 million. The sale's closing was contingent upon Flying J and Shell reaching an agreement with the U.S. Environmental Protection Agency and the Department of Justice. Additionally, Flying J was required to file a petition with the San Joaquin Valley Air Pollution Control District for a variance to State of California air quality criteria. The Flying J team wasn't concerned about meeting environmental requirements. They were confident the State of California would work with them.

In March 2005, the San Joaquin Valley Air Pollution Control District granted Flying J a one-year extension to comply with its emissions rule. Shell Oil and Flying J signed the final paperwork for the sale and the facility was officially Flying J's.

Flying J struggled to turn a profit at the refinery, which was operated by Flying J's subsidiary Big West. Though the refinery was pumping out fuel, it never reached its maximum processing rate of 70,000 barrels of oil per day due to lack of crude oil, outdated equipment, and political uncertainties. The refinery's production peaked at about 83 percent of capacity and plummeted as low as 50 percent. High oil prices, inclement weather, and refinery outages limited production. It was a disappointment to Flying J, as well as to those who thought it would help the California fuel demand.

Though acquiring the Bakersfield Refinery came with several risks, Flying J executives believed the pros would eventually outweigh the cons. Although Shell executives had argued that they lacked affordable crude oil to refine, Flying J saw a potential advantage in the mere proximity of the refinery to what crude oil there was in the area. The close proximity meant Flying J would incur less freight expense than coastal refineries, which also meant Flying J could sell its product to the market at a lower cost. The refinery's seemingly significant location advantage allowed Flying J executives to turn their focus to improving the refinery's outdated structure.

But the company first had to overcome one glaring problem: it lacked a guaranteed supply of crude oil. Industry experts knew that buying a refinery without a crude supply was more than risky business—it could easily lead to the downfall of the refinery. Yet Flying J executives remained confident. They believed they had contracted for enough oil prior to the acquisition to keep the refinery up and running while they secured additional supplies. But they discovered that they couldn't access much of the nearby oil, which would have provided them their hoped-for freight expense advantage, as it was already locked up in supply agreements with competing refiners.

Flying J hit another hurdle when it lost Jeff Utley, a key Big West executive who had been with the company for years, in a tragic motorcycle accident on August 5, 2005. For years Jeff was the company's go-to executive on multiple fronts. His official title was senior vice president for refining, but he was much more to the company and its employees. He was a particularly talented negotiator and problem solver—skills he brought to Bakersfield as it attempted to navigate the many roadblocks impeding its success. After the Bakersfield acquisition, Jeff split his time between the North Salt Lake Refinery and Bakersfield. His goal was to keep employees happy and operations running smoothly—a feat he accomplished, considering the setbacks that were out of Flying J's control.

Jeff was a key figure in the company's community relations, in addition to playing an essential role in keeping employees engaged. North Salt Lake and Bakersfield refinery employees loved Jeff. He had the unique ability to get everyone moving in the same direction, regardless of the challenges facing the company.

Upon his passing, employee relations became more difficult. The Bakersfield Refinery had a drastically different culture than the North Salt Lake Refinery, and while Jeff was a master at keeping the two employee groups happy, employee engagement quickly deteriorated without his presence. He knew the California Air Resources Board (CARB) better than anyone else in the company. With his passing, relations between Bakersfield and CARB diminished.

When Flying J acquired Bakersfield, the refinery lacked the ability to convert heavy oils into gasoline and diesel fuels that could legally be used by land vehicles, including everyday cars and trucks. The refinery's structure was so outdated that its refined product couldn't pass California's stringent environmental regulations. Bakersfield primarily produced bunker fuel that could be sold to ships in the marine industry. Overall, the refinery needed significant upgrades to be compliant in the future, which put Bakersfield at a serious disadvantage.

The inability to produce fuel that everyday consumers could pump into their cars and trucks proved to be a huge obstacle, and it quickly became a top priority to solve. By early 2006, Big West and Flying J execs knew that the refinery needed to be upgraded to meet industry and regulatory standards. Ultimately, the refinery's success depended on its ability to convert less valuable hydrocarbon products into highly valued gasoline and diesel fuel.

Jeff had also been extremely instrumental in the Clean Fuels Project that was envisioned to make Bakersfield an efficient and profitable operation. The project included two plans. Plan A was to revamp the refinery with updated technology that could convert crude oil into high-value California-compliant gasoline, known as CARB gasoline. At the time, Bakersfield was creating *some* CARB gasoline and diesel, but it made too much product that was *not* gasoline and diesel, including ship fuel and asphalt. The project was intended to convert most of that product into gasoline and diesel.

Though the best option, Plan A came with limitations, with environmental regulations again being the key hurdle. At the time, converting the dirtier, heavier, and less desirable products into much-needed, high-value CARB gasoline required the use of controversial chemicals—chemicals that the public and environmental advocates loudly opposed. Though many believed the chemicals used to refine CARB gasoline would actually have fewer adverse environmental implications than continuing the status quo, others viewed the use of the chemicals as a major impediment to the state's clean energy efforts. Public opposition to those chemicals grew, and Flying J eventually decided to put Plan A to rest.

In many ways Plan B, which focused on producing high-value diesel fuel, made more sense. Diesel was priced higher than gasoline, and demand for diesel fuel was on the rise. Moreover, demand wasn't just growing in California or the West; it was growing throughout North America. It quickly became clear that producing high-value diesel fuel was the best option for the struggling refinery. Big West executives tried pushing Plan B forward fast. But again, roadblocks slowed their progress.

Flying J wasn't the only company to recognize the huge potential the diesel fuel market presented. Competing coastal refineries were anxious to get on the diesel-producing bandwagon, and a supply competition among the refiners was in full swing.

Several refineries—including Bakersfield—needed to upgrade their infrastructure before they could develop the high-value diesel product. Before long, several refineries were on a talent hunt, competing for the country's top engineers and manufacturers, as well as manufacturing equipment. Flying J knew it needed skilled engineers who could upgrade Bakersfield to be able to convert those heavy oils into diesel fuels. They didn't have a choice—diesel was the refinery's only viable option.

Flying J competed fiercely for the country's best engineers. It needed this project to be successful—the refinery's long-term success depended on it. But it also needed the capital to make it happen. Flying J met with Bank of America and explained its needs and the potential to dominate the diesel market. Bank of America came on board and signed a large financial deal that would fund the Bakersfield upgrade.

Bank of America's $800 million loan was the largest loan Flying J had ever entered into for a singular purpose. The loan included detailed language regarding its purpose, which was to expand the Bakersfield Refinery and to manage its working capital of inventories. With the loan in hand, the refinery would have adequate cash to upgrade its aging facility and develop a dynamic production schedule. Ultimately the loan ensured the refinery had sufficient cash flow to operate in the robust diesel fuel market.

Flying J embarked on an ambitious expansion and infrastructure plan that exceeded $800 million—more than six times the $130 million Flying J paid for the refinery. The plan called for new equipment and upgrades that would increase the refinery's oil-processing capacity and significantly squeeze more gasoline from each barrel of crude. When completed, the expansion would double the plant's diesel output by as early as mid-2008.

While it began investing in the expansion, Flying J awaited permits from the San Joaquin Valley Air Pollution Control District. The district had yet to approve Flying J's plans to produce diesel fuel. Fred Greener, our president of refining after Jeff's passing, worked with his team for years with Kern County to try to get the permits through the California regulatory system to be able to build the needed process equipment, but it faced delay after delay. Still confident that the permits would eventually be approved, Flying J moved forward at the recommendations of its engineers and manufacturers. Construction began on the new plant design, and everyone was excited to begin a new phase at Bakersfield. Using the Bank of America loan, Flying J invested close to $600 million in Plan B before ever receiving the green light from the State of California. Fred finally had the permit in hand in December 2008.

He had a celebratory dinner in Bakersfield and flew home to Utah, only to find out that Flying J would be filing for bankruptcy in a few days and that it was likely the much anticipated upgrades would never happen.

Celebration

Flying J had seen several years of tremendous growth and success. One thing we had never done was celebrate this success with our high-level executives. In late 2007, I cornered Phil and told him it was time to take key executives and their spouses on the trip of a lifetime to say thanks.

In late September 2008, just as the country was stepping into the Great Recession, we boarded a luxury cruise ship in Venice and set sail across the Adriatic Sea. It was an extravagant, weeklong escape. As we made our way from Italy to Croatia to Greece, we spent our days enveloped in the turquoise sea and surrounded by the Mediterranean's exotic beauty, amazing history and artifacts, and relaxing atmosphere. It was a perfect getaway. It was a great way to show our appreciation for years of service from an executive team who had been an integral part of Flying J's success. We took time to reflect on our past successes and imagine all that we could accomplish together in the future. I asked everyone to tell their favorite Flying J story. My brother, Thad, shared a great story about flying across the country with my dad in a helicopter and stopping at Flying J plazas along the way—some that had Thad's Restaurants in them. Everyone laughed as Thad, for whom the restaurants were named, told how one plaza employee asked for his autograph and didn't even recognize our dad. It was a great evening of reminiscing. The optimistic spirit and can-do energy flowed through the team. We all had tremendous pride and confidence in Flying J.

Flying J executives and spouses enjoy gelato in Venice, Italy, celebrating years of success, September 2008.

But as the saying often goes, hindsight is 20/20. We were all well aware that the United States was entering an economic slowdown, and we knew that oil prices were on the decline, but I didn't realize the magnitude of the situation we would soon be facing. Flying J wasn't as strong as it appeared. The company was entering turbulent times with dark days on the horizon.

As we ended our weeklong Mediterranean excursion, I knew that the economy was faltering, but I was confident that the phenomenal executive team with Phil at the reins would lead us through it. Even though at the time I was on the board of directors and not working in the trenches with them, I was so proud of what they had accomplished. I knew that my dad would have been proud too.

We stepped off the cruise ship and right back into reality. We had left on the cruise knowing that the global economy was struggling. Prior to our getaway we had watched as historic companies like Lehman Brothers collapsed. The markets had crashed and continued on a downward trend.

On October 6, 2008, the Dow closed below 10,000 points for the first time since 2004, and by the end of the month most financial markets had lost 30 percent of their value. Phrases like mortgage crisis, banking collapse, and government bailouts became commonplace. Everyone was nervous. No one knew what to expect next.

Chuck and I sensed that times were changing and we realized we needed to divest our property in Gulfport, Mississippi. In 2005 we had experienced unexpected high returns at the Gulfport Crystal Inn when Hurricane Katrina hit the area. This was one of the few Flying J sites that we built next to. Our hotel sustained $1.6 million worth of damage, but since it sat on a hill it did not get impacted as much and the damage was not enough to close the hotel. Since it was located only 10 miles from the major disaster site, the hotel ran completely full for three years housing out-of-town people helping with the cleanup. Other properties had been rebuilt and Gulfport businesses were headed back to their prehurricane level of returns. It was time to sell. We knew the economy was struggling, so we looked at real estate locations where we thought the economy would stay strong enough to do a 1031 exchange for our hotel property, which would allow us to defer taxes on capital gains. We ended up selling the Gulfport property in October 2008 for a great price. We used the proceeds to buy two apartments in Manhattan. As my dad believed, luck is always part of the mix. We were lucky to get out of the Gulfport property when we did, and our New York City investments continue to perform.

Things were not going as smoothly at Flying J. Crude oil prices were also dropping—and they were dropping fast. From 2005 to 2008, crude prices had experienced steady increases. In 2006, crude oil traded for a then record high of $79 per barrel. The upward trend continued over the next years, reaching $92 a barrel by October 2007 and surpassing $100 in January 2008. The steady increase continued over the next several months, reaching $117 per barrel in April and $138 in June, with prices peaking at $148 in July 2008. But as the national economy tanked, crude oil prices started to plummet. By September, crude had dropped to $100 per barrel. And it kept falling, hitting $64 in October and $60 in November, and plummeting to a dismal $32 a barrel in December.

From my perspective, the only economic concern at Flying J was crude prices falling and the inventory losses we were incurring. In November, as I reviewed the financials, there was good news and bad news. Retail had a stellar month. Revenues were still increasing and we had lots of cash coming in. The bad news was that the Bakersfield Refinery and Longhorn Pipeline were losing money.

By late 2008, the Longhorn Pipeline and the Bakersfield Refinery had combined inventories of several million barrels of oil, gasoline, and diesel fuels. Despite the large product quantity, the assets were never adequately protected from market price risk with hedging instruments. And as the industry faced the downward spiral of prices in the third and fourth quarters of 2008, Flying J's daily inventory losses exceeded $10 million on many occasions. Market conditions were destroying the value of the inventory that the two systems required to be able to operate. Neither of them were operating with sufficient profit to restore the cash availability needed to continue their operation.

Flying J was bound to lose millions of dollars during the next few months. And with crude prices plummeting we were feeling a serious cash pinch. Cash was leaving the company to meet obligations faster than it was coming in. Furthermore, I learned that we had only partially hedged our crude oil, and that we had sold those hedges in October when crude fell to $64 per barrel. We sold the hedges too early under the assumption that prices wouldn't fall any further, but they did. By selling our hedges in October, we essentially lost our insurance policy against the falling prices. With the world's economy in shambles, crude prices dropping, and two underperforming assets, Flying J was headed for a crisis.

On December 8, 2008, I attended the Flying J management meeting and learned that outside of the Longhorn Pipeline and Bakersfield Refinery, the company was actually on track. In fact, Flying J was on pace to hit $20 billion in revenue—the second most profitable year in its history. I addressed the management group, thanking them for their efforts, and letting them know annual bonuses would go out as planned. I left the room breathing a sigh of relief—while the picture wasn't bright, I believed we'd get through this hard time like we had before. In hindsight this proved to be too early, because crude prices continued to fall.

On my way out I had a quick chat with Flying J's legal counsel. I had planned for the first time to sell some stock—Chuck and I were beginning a house renovation.

"Phil cut off stock transactions," counsel informed me, with a tone that implied he thought I knew.

In the past, Flying J had always purchased stock back at the employee's request, so counsel's comment seemed odd. I was confused about the situation and wondered, "Why would a billion-dollar company stop stock transactions among its employees?" I decided to drop by the controller's office.

"What's going on? Why have stock transactions been suspended?" I asked him out of curiosity rather than skepticism. "It's hard to believe that a billion-dollar company can't pay out a few million to our employees."

He told me he couldn't conduct any stock transactions—he was too worried about cash flow. Our December crude bill was due on December 20, and he was openly nervous about how we would have the cash to pay it.

I spent the rest of the day at Flying J talking to people who might have had an idea of what was going on. I needed to figure out why stock transactions had stopped. I gathered information from individuals who were in the process of selling stock, and I realized that only a few had made requests, amounting to around $5 million total. I couldn't understand why we couldn't pay out $5 million—it just didn't add up. I was starting to get nervous. In my gut I knew something was wrong.

My next stop was Phil's office. He quickly confirmed that stock transactions had been suspended. But that's about all he said. I also didn't say much—I was still shocked and confused. I asked him about the Longhorn Pipeline and the Bakersfield Refinery. I said I thought he should consider cutting back on throughput until crude prices stabilized. And that was the end of our discussion. I trusted Phil's leadership and believed he knew what was best. He would make the necessary decisions to keep Flying J moving forward.

I called Chuck on the way home and told him that Phil had stopped all stock transactions, including what we were requesting. Chuck was furious. Like me, he said it made no sense. Chuck and I had a long discussion late into the night.

I met with Thad first thing the next morning and informed him about the stock buyback being suspended. I told him I wasn't quite sure what was going on. Like Chuck and me, Thad was upset and confused—he agreed that it simply didn't add up. We decided it was time to meet with Phil.

As I arrived at Flying J, I decided to dig a little further before discussing the stock situation with Phil. I didn't like what I discovered. Phil had taken out a $3.5 million loan from the company. I knew that he had taken out loans in the past, but what caught me off guard was that Phil hadn't signed a promissory note, something he understandably demanded of everyone, including Thad and me.

I was conflicted. Phil had cut off everyone else from selling stock, but then took out a loan for himself. Again, the story didn't add up.

Thad and I met with Phil to get to the bottom of what was happening. He explained that with crude prices dropping and two of our assets, Longhorn Pipeline and Bakersfield Refinery, losing cash, the company simply couldn't afford to pay out to employees requesting a stock buyout. I left Phil's office outwardly calm, but I was fuming inside. It was obvious that I was completely out of the loop.

Later that evening I met with our former CFO, Scott Clayson, and his wife for dinner. He had recently resigned from the company in July, but he still had a handle on Flying J's inner workings. He had played a strong watchdog role in the company, which we lost with his departure. Fortunately I still had a close relationship with him and knew I could depend on him for advice. He was shocked by the news and adamant that we get in touch with our bank lending partners to let them know we were in trouble. He felt confident given the situation that they would work with us.

The next day I was approached by the Longhorn Pipeline CFO with disturbing information. He explained that the $800 million loan proceeds that Bank of America had provided to Big West for the purpose of expanding and operating the Bakersfield Refinery were all being indirectly used to support the Longhorn Pipeline. Evidently the Bank of America loan was the only access to liquidity that Flying J had to maintain sufficient cash flow to operate in the wake of excessive losses due to crude prices falling. He had been told that Thad and I were well aware of the situation and to follow Phil's directions. But his department couldn't in good conscience sign a document stating that all was in compliance. We had been misusing the funds—we were out of covenant.

Without our financial officers' signatures, Bank of America investigated and quickly discovered that the loan had been misused for several months, funding activities outside of the refinery. But during that time, as the nation's economy was tumbling, many banks were working with companies to prevent bankruptcy and defaults. Bank of America was willing to work with Flying J. They developed a plan that included funding the company under much tighter supervision and allocating a penalty interest rate. However, Phil was unwilling to meet their demands or bring it to the attention of the board of directors. Instead he rebutted their plan and attempted to call their bluff. Perhaps he didn't believe that the bank would push Flying J into bankruptcy. Unaware of these issues, I was focused on the potential cash flow issues, not understanding how bad things really were.

Preparing for Bankruptcy

Principle: Honesty and trust are essential to leadership.

On December 16, 2008, I was Christmas shopping while awaiting a phone call from Phil. For the past two weeks my head had been spinning with all the news indicating that Flying J was in a serious bind, but I had no clue how serious the situation was. I was aware there was an important call with Bank of America that morning, and Phil had promised he would call with an update. To kill time I had headed to the store to purchase a wakeboard for my kids for Christmas. When Phil called, he told me that Bank of America was on board to issue a credit waiver to us.

"This is all going to be fine," Phil reassured me.

Our legal counsel, who knew I was worried about our loan from Bank of America, called me just seconds after I'd hung up with Phil.

"Bank of America is asking who our bankruptcy attorneys are," he said.

Time stopped, and in my mind I still connect that wakeboard with the moment I was told that Flying J was filing for bankruptcy. I was paralyzed. Bankruptcy. I repeated the word over and over in my head. I couldn't think of what to say. Just minutes before, Phil had reassured me that everything was fine.

"Bankruptcy?" I questioned.

"Yes, it's likely we will have to file within a week." It was obvious our legal counsel was in shock too and looking for direction.

I took a deep breath and exhaled. Was I dreaming? Bankruptcy. That had to be a mistake. How could this be happening? I had never imagined that Flying J would reach this state. What was going on?

"I'm going to have to call you back," I told him. I could hear the confusion and disbelief in my voice as we said good-bye. None of this made sense.

I took a few more breaths and called Phil. He picked up on the first ring.

"Don't worry, Crystal. I have this under control," he said without even saying hello.

As usual, Phil was confident he'd work out a deal with Bank of America and we wouldn't have to file. The bankruptcy paperwork was precautionary, he said. He knew that Bank of America, who had been our financial partner for years and had funded our loan to revamp the Bakersfield Refinery, would support us. Phil was about to board the company plane to fly to Washington, D.C., for a business-as-usual meeting with a potential business partner. He wasn't even planning to meet with Bank of America, who was on the brink of throwing us into bankruptcy if we did not cooperate with their request!

I was at a loss as to what to do. Our crude bill was coming due in a few days and we didn't have the necessary cash to pay it. We needed Bank of America to work with us. We needed $120 million to pay the crude bill by Friday—just a few days away—or we would have to file for Chapter 11.

I didn't get much rest that night. The thought that Flying J—a company on *Forbes*'s list of the 100 largest private businesses in America, a company with 15,000 employees, a company with revenues exceeding $20 billion, my dad's company—could be filing Chapter 11 made me sick. I couldn't wrap my head around what was happening. I knew I needed to take action. Even though Phil was the CEO, Flying J was still a private family-owned company, and now Thad and I were *the* family. More than mere members of the board of directors, we owned 85 percent of the stock at the time. It was shocking to know that the bank had been misled by Phil while Thad and I were led to believe all was well. We had no idea the company at the time was in such deep trouble. To make matters worse, the other 15 percent of the stock was held by an ESOP (employee stock ownership plan) and other executives who had trusted their livelihood to Flying J.

Phil's vision to build a giant gas and oil retailer that would eventually control freight was an enormous undertaking. Every division and subsidiary of the company played a crucial role in reaching the objective. From TAB and TCH to the travel plazas, Phil wanted to turn Flying J and all its services into a one-stop shop for trucking owner/operators. He wanted drivers to rely on Flying J for all their needs—from conducting business and operations to having an improved quality of life on the road. The plan seemed flawless.

Phil probably thought oil prices would surge back up. And *had* oil prices turned upward, Flying J's credit line, which was based on the price of oil, would have been maintained. As long as crude oil maintained its price, the company didn't owe anything; but every time the price dropped, a loan payment had to be made.

As Flying J entered bankruptcy at the close of 2008, the company had incurred inventory losses of over $300 million from the Bakersfield Refinery and Longhorn Pipeline. The retail facilities and the profitable North Salt Lake Refinery could not shoulder all of the company's cash needs. Furthermore, the company was not financed in a way that allowed cash to move from one company to another, due to existing siloed loan covenants. So even though one division may have had cash to spare, it could not be used to pay down loans in other divisions. Loan balances were also high due to all the capital costs put forward for the Bakersfield Refinery upgrade.

While there's no doubt that Flying J's acquisitions of the Bakersfield Refinery and Longhorn Pipeline played a critical role in its bankruptcy, the company overall saw great levels of success, with sales growing from $4.4 billion in 2000 to $18.6 billion in 2008. Flying J was praised for being one of the trucking industry's most innovative companies. In many ways the company was at the top of its game. It was moving forward fast, and seemingly nothing could slow it down. It was an exciting time to be at Flying J. Positive energy and motivation filled the company. It seemed as if it were moving in only one direction: up. There was always a push to say, "What else can we do? How can we be better and stronger?" Phil had taken Jay's bustling company and grown it far beyond what Jay ever thought possible.

Phil and Jay were both phenomenal entrepreneurs and visionaries. They were the type of people who could roll up their sleeves and turn hard work into results. While they shared these entrepreneurial traits, they were vastly different leaders. Phil was a financial mastermind. He wanted to try different approaches and take risks—risks that didn't always pay off. Phil demanded growth at an accelerated pace and pushed hard for innovation. He would dictate what he expected to see accomplished, and his word was final.

Jay was a real estate guru—he could spot a good deal from a mile away. Unlike Phil, he wanted his employees to run the show. He entrusted them with autonomy to manage their work and departments. He didn't want to hand-hold them or oversee their every move. When Jay passed away, Phil's management style became even more demanding. He no longer had Jay to answer to. Thad and I would question some of his decisions, but Phil was very strategic. He always had a plan that sounded doable, and he had a way of convincing you that the future was bright. I'm not sure whether he ever respected our wishes or ideas. I was a significant stockholder and a board member, yet when I'd question whether a decision made sense I'd hear the same response from the executive team: "Phil knows what he's doing."

In retrospect I think people were fearful and timid, yet despite their fear they believed in Phil and his vision. They saw him as a leader who would take the company to a higher place; that anything he touched would turn to gold. My dad had taught us to trust and respect Phil. Jay's absence left Phil with no real mentor or advisor, nor anyone to hold him accountable. He had also lost a close friend and confidant in Buzz Germer, who was with my dad in the plane crash. It got even worse a few years later when refining VP Jeff Utley was killed. Phil was left to make decisions without a peer group to help balance his ambitious goals.

Under Phil's direction the company was constantly trying to stay ahead of the competition, aiming to be the industry's trailblazer. There was always something new to accomplish or a company to acquire, with little concern for risk management. But while Flying J was seemingly on a path to even greater success, there seemed to be no recognition that the company also needed adequate cash flow to sustain those opportunities. Phil was focused on market share and top-line revenue, believing that a larger market share would create significant leverage and opportunities, and create a long-term advantage. Some projects were started and left unfinished, or launched before they were ready. There was never enough time to look back and examine what worked and what didn't work—Phil required everyone's attention to be focused forward, never looking back on the past.

Since I knew we were now in crisis mode, I was determined to keep moving forward. I wasn't sure of the necessary steps we needed to take, but I knew we had to figure it out and take them. At that point there was nothing I could do, so I did my best to shake the bankruptcy from my mind. I decided to brave the Christmas rush and take my twins shopping, as I had promised long before I knew of the bankruptcy. I knew it wouldn't be fun, but maybe it would distract me for a little while, so I went through the motions. I was wrong. Trying to avoid the situation was impossible, and soon I was on the phone again reaching out to trusted friends for advice and help.

I called the chairman of Zions Bancorporation. Zions had always been a helpful lender to Flying J over the years, and we had an unsecured credit line with the bank. I knew the chairman would offer sound advice, even if he couldn't provide any financial aid. I explained Flying J's situation while my daughters wailed excitedly in the background at all the fun finds they discovered. Perhaps it wasn't the best time to have this sensitive discussion, but I went for it. It was surreal to watch my daughters' excitement when I was so paralyzed with worry. Like everyone else, he was shocked.

"What can I do to help?" he asked.

He listened thoughtfully as I explained the pinch we were in. He spoke slowly and carefully as he explained that our unsecured credit line was maxed out. And considering the nation's current economic conditions, there was nothing Zions could do for us.

"My hands are tied," he said. "I suggest you hire the best high-profile legal team you can find." Later that week I would take his advice.

As each hour passed, I knew we were getting closer and closer to filing. I couldn't stand by and watch, leaving the company's fate in Phil's hands—I needed to do something. I reached out to our former CFO, Scott Clayson, again, and I was glad I had secured him earlier in the year to be our family advisor. He didn't flinch when I asked him for help. He was willing to help without a second thought.

He jumped right in, scheduling meetings with banks on the East Coast to raise money. Before I knew it, he was joining Thad, me, and the current Flying J controller on a red-eye flight to New York. I was nervous. Everyone was used to working with Phil. I rarely represented the company and worried I lacked credibility. To make matters worse, Thad had fallen into an alcohol addiction over the past few years and I was concerned that he would get to New York and just find a bar. But there was too much on the line to focus on my fears. I needed to do all I could to keep us from filing for bankruptcy.

We landed in New York at 5 a.m. and I called Phil, who was still in Washington, D.C., to let him know about our meetings. Since he had the company jet and was so close, I was hopeful he would join us in New York for the bank talks.

"It looks like you have it under control," he said, opting to fly back to Utah. I didn't understand why he seemed so callous about the situation. We had never undergone anything like this. What could possibly be more important? It was critical that we were all on the same side, working in the same direction. Yet Phil didn't want to engage, or at least it seemed that way.

Thad stayed committed to helping me, and our first meeting was with ING Bank. We couldn't pay our crude bill. And the price was high; we needed $120 million by Friday, December 20.

ING was optimistic—it was evident they thought they could help, and even more importantly they *wanted* to help. We spent hours on end at the ING office exploring our options. By the end of the day ING had a plan to offer assistance, but the plan depended on whether Bank of America would relinquish us from being out of covenant. We had several other bank lenders that had provided Flying J and its subsidiaries with revolving credit lines in the past join a conference call with Bank of America—our largest lender at the time—to show support for our unique situation. We were hopeful.

But Bank of America wasn't happy with the terms ING helped us create. In fact, they weren't happy with us at all. After all, Flying J had broken its covenant on the Bank of America loan; they confirmed that they were aware we had been transferring cash from the Bakersfield Refinery loan to pay off the Longhorn Pipeline loan, an action that was expressly prohibited. Bank of America was furious with our actions, and I couldn't blame them. I was horrifically embarrassed. We decided to take time to regroup and scheduled another call for the next day.

As we left ING, I called Flying J's Accounting Department. I needed everyone working for as long as it took to pull together all facts about our Bank of America loan. Bank of America wanted answers about exactly how the funds had been used. We needed to be armed with all the information for tomorrow's call so we could tell them exactly what had happened.

My next call was to Phil, who wasn't very happy that I was speaking to Bank of America. In fact, he adamantly requested that I didn't talk to them again. He wanted me out of it. Phil's reaction worried me. He still seemed undisturbed by this terrible situation. From my perspective we were running out of options, and December 20—the day our $120 million crude bill was due—was only two days away. It appeared that Phil did not have a plan.

The next day I reluctantly stayed off the conference call with

Bank of America per Phil's request. I knew everybody was prepared and ready to face the fire. And who knew, maybe Bank of America would work with us if they were told exactly what had happened. Banks all over the country were working with companies in situations similar to ours. At least we had that on our side.

I anxiously awaited news from the call, but when I finally heard what happened I wasn't happy. The call didn't go well. Phil decided that he didn't want to disclose the financial information Bank of America had requested. I truly believe Phil thought Bank of America would eventually give in. I didn't think—and I believe *Phil* didn't think—that they would let us default on the loan, but that's the direction they were leaning.

My panic was growing. Though Phil was the CEO, my family owned the company and would ultimately be responsible for the outcome of this crisis. So while still in New York, I began to focus my attention on finding a strong legal team instead of a bank to help us get out of this mess. My small team met with Kirkland & Ellis, a law firm with a nationally acclaimed bankruptcy practice that had been recommended by one of the banks we had met with. I set up an appointment, and within 45 minutes we were in their offices discussing our situation with the firm's restructuring partners.

Almost immediately I knew we were in good hands. It was obvious that the Kirkland & Ellis team was the right fit for our unique needs. I felt a surge of confidence. We stayed with them until 2 a.m., working through the next several steps we needed to take. Despite a long night, they hit the ground running first thing the next morning.

Kirkland & Ellis facilitated one more call with Bank of America, hoping they would restructure the loan with Flying J rather than force us into bankruptcy. Although Bank of America was happy Kirkland was working on our behalf, they felt too betrayed to work with us—it was too late. Bank of America pulled the plug. Phil wasn't willing to accept their terms of tighter supervision and a penalty interest fee, so their only option was to stop working with us. And with Bank of America no longer on our side, we were in big trouble. We had no choice but to make the announcement I was dreading.

Our work was done in New York and we flew home Friday knowing that on Monday morning we would be announcing bankruptcy. There was still much work needed to prepare for an awful announcement just a few days before Christmas. Thad had accompanied me to New York, but that would be the last time he would actively participate in moving the company forward or our reorganization plan. Only a few days later he relinquished his position as chairman of the board to me, becoming a supportive board member and brother, but not engaging in the day-to-day work to reorganize the company.

On Monday, December 22, 2008, smack in the middle of the holiday season, we announced that Flying J was filing for Chapter 11 bankruptcy. When I arrived back in Utah, Chuck and I sat down with our four children (all under the age of 13) to explain the situation. I didn't want to scare them and assured them we would be fine. But I also wanted to impart the seriousness of Flying J's bankruptcy. I had tried to always be there for them, just as I promised myself I *would* be long before I ever had children. I wanted to be the kind of mom who put her family first, but now it seemed there was a bigger purpose. Many families' lives were at stake, not just mine. I hoped my young children would understand. I was putting our family name and business in front of my role as mother.

After explaining Flying J's dire situation as best we could, I looked for assurance that my children would understand how we as a family would be affected. I wanted them to understand that I would be gone a lot—way more than they were used to. I had hoped they would understand, but their young, innocent faces stared back at me with doubt. They *didn't* understand. For their entire lives I had been close at hand, supporting their dreams, successes, and failures. Now at 44 years old, my focus as a devoted stay-at-home mom switched to managing the survival of Flying J. A lot of tears were shed, including my own. Flashbacks to my own childhood flooded my mind. I remember so well my mom suddenly starting to work and how hard the transition had been for me.

I hoped my children would be more supportive than I had been for my mother, and it was reassuring to me that they had one big advantage—their dad was available to them. I think it helped that Chuck and I had always kept the children in the know with what was happening. Even though they were caught off guard with the bankruptcy just as we were, they understood that I had to now unexpectedly be away more than I ever had before. I know I had promised myself that I would not put work before family, but this was short term, important to my extended family, and I felt if I kept the kids updated on what was happening it may prove to be a good learning experience for them at a young age.

At that moment I believed it would be temporary. I told them six months—just until we got things sorted out and did what was right to pay creditors back and keep our employees' jobs. I needed to save the family name. At the time I had no idea this would drag out indefinitely, bringing numerous nannies and teachers into my children's lives and certainly testing the patience of my husband. As I continued changing from one hat to another, I would commonly ask how my children were handling the work situation. I was well aware of how I had felt when my mother would rush out the door to yet another meeting, and even if my children didn't speak their mind as I had, I still had a sense of guilt for abandoning them. Chuck stepped up and was more than capable of supporting me and the kids.

The Real Work Begins

From that moment on I never quit working to exit bankruptcy successfully. I was ready and willing to do whatever it took to get out of this mess. No longer would I be sitting on the sidelines watching as the company unraveled. It was like a Harvard case study brought before the class to analyze. The only difference was this case wasn't going to end when the class hour was over. The decisions made were going to affect thousands of lives, and the employment of thousands of employees.

We had arrived back home from New York late Friday night, December 19, and everyone worked around the clock to ensure we had a plan in place by Monday morning.

Within those few short days we had hired Kirkland & Ellis, our legal team; The Blackstone Group, our financial advisor; and Kekst, our PR firm. Though everything was a mess, I was optimistic they would help solve our problems.

Those next few days were a blur. I spent every waking hour talking through the bankruptcy with Flying J executives and our outside counsel. Decisions had to be made immediately. I was running from fire to fire. Chuck was also working full-time to help understand our cash situation. Christmas came and went with all the same family traditions, like our annual family Christmas Eve party. I wanted to protect the kids as much as I could, but it was difficult to celebrate in such turbulent times.

Our executive teams and employees were in disbelief and shock. They had left work on Friday thinking all was fine, and Monday morning they came into a completely different situation with no real warning. In the first few days everyone pulled together to help in any way they could to keep the companies operating, but futures were unclear and career dreams did not look bright. I spent my days talking with our employees about the situation, reassuring them that I would do my best to make things right. From our executive teams to employees on the ground, no one knew what would come next. Employee morale had taken a beating.

Many of our divisions were not part of the bankruptcy, and they needed direction that they were not getting. Each of the divisions had to stand on their own as if they were a separate company; we could not use cash from one company to help another company. From the day we filed bankruptcy, we had to pay all our vendors up front, so we had to make enough money from operations to purchase all crude, fuel, and restaurant supplies on a daily basis, before they were ever delivered to us.

I held a management meeting. I wanted the executives to know that we were all in this together. I tried to impart a sense of urgency and optimism. I told them to focus on running their divisions and to stop any ancillary projects that were consuming and not generating cash. I needed everyone focused and making smart decisions. I asked them to examine their departments and think of ways to save time and money. I trusted them, and I wanted them to know it. It was clear that my dad's philosophy of hiring good people and then letting them run their departments had gotten lost over the past several years. In my opinion there was no way that Phil or I could know as much about their departments as they did. It was time to put control back in their hands. I wanted to again be a *team* of leaders, not just one leader at the top.

Everyone had a different reaction to the crisis. Some of the employees were paralyzed with fear; others were motivated to work even harder. There were employees who had mortgaged their homes to buy company stock, and now the banks would likely demand payment. Other than tell them I was doing the best I could, I couldn't really advise them. I didn't know what was going to happen. Their panic pushed me further into go mode. We needed to move fast, and we needed to make decisions now. Phil couldn't make the decisions that needed to be made. It seemed as though he were in shock. He had always been such a strong, smart leader, but now he wasn't acting like the confident leader I knew.

Soon after Christmas it became obvious that we needed to close the Bakersfield Refinery. We did not have the cash flow to continue to buy enough crude to keep the refinery operating. The multimillion-dollar upgrade that we had engineered and purchased equipment to complete would likely never happen, even though we had finally received permits. We needed to shut it down, at least for the time being.

The Longhorn Pipeline was also holding us back. We decided to ship only to third parties to save costs. But we quickly realized that we needed to either sell Longhorn or find a partner, which wasn't a promising solution. Something had to change at both Bakersfield and Longhorn. We couldn't support these endeavors. After much discussion, it was decided to put Longhorn up for sale and to stop processing crude oil at the Bakersfield Refinery.

Another step was to meet with ConocoPhillips, which had been one of our long-standing partners since forming the CFJ joint venture in the early 1990s. ConocoPhillips was also one of our largest fuel suppliers, which now made them a major creditor in our bankruptcy. Now that we had no credit with any vendors, ConocoPhillips was our only short-term hope to continue supplying fuel to our retail facilities. However, due to earlier disagreements about how the retail business was managed, our relationship with ConocoPhillips was already strained and they had no interest in working with us.

Phil spelled out the situation to them, explaining both our immediate needs and yearlong budgetary needs. They came on board to help us get through the next several weeks until the dust settled. But they wanted collateral to secure liabilities that arose prior to Flying J filing bankruptcy. Phil was adamantly opposed. He didn't want to give them anything. I, on the other hand, thought we needed to consider their request. It wasn't the time to be bargaining.

In the end, Phil agreed to give them first right to dividend payments from the CFJ partnership and the ability to sell off properties if we couldn't pay them back. This agreement was critical to keep us operating.

Beyond cash, what Flying J needed most was to heal our damaged reputation and internal morale. Everyone was nervous about our future, but I couldn't let anyone—our employees, creditors, or industry competitors—think Flying J was not going to pay back its incredible debt. I spent countless hours talking with whomever needed a boost of confidence. I knew that it was essential to keep spirits up. I believed we still had a valuable company and we would do what was needed to make it right.

By the middle of January we had hired a temporary chief restructuring officer (CRO), John Boken. This seasoned executive was to help lead us through Chapter 11, but I knew it would take time for him to get up to speed. It was becoming clearer and clearer to me that there was no one person leading the entire company. I had lost confidence and trust in Phil's leadership. I wanted direction for our executives and they were not getting it.

From Phil's personal loan to going out of covenant with Bank of America, too many questionable decisions had been made under his leadership. I wanted to lay everything out on the table. There was no point in tiptoeing around the issue. I respect open, honest communication, so I decided to have a candid conversation with Phil.

"I don't trust you anymore," I said bluntly to him.

"Then I need to quit, Crystal. I've never said anything to you that I didn't believe myself," he replied.

"Let's sleep on this and talk more tomorrow," I said. He walked out without saying another word. That was the last time I saw Phil.

I never intended for a seemingly simple conversation to be the end of Phil's leadership tenure with the company. My dad had always trusted Phil, and while I had questioned some of his decisions over the years, I had been groomed to follow his lead.

Still, I never anticipated what happened the next morning as I was driving to the office and noticed Phil was calling.

"Crystal," he said, "I'm not coming back."

My jaw dropped. Never in a million years did I expect to hear a resignation come from Phil. He was so committed to the company. Flying J was his life.

But at the same time I knew it was the right decision. The risks he took had cost us too much. It was time for new leadership to lead the company in a different direction. I accepted his resignation.

Without putting the phone down I called Chuck.

"Phil's gone. He just resigned. He's not coming back."

Chuck was just as shocked as I was, but also agreed that his departure was for the best. From that point forward, the future of the company's 10 subsidiaries and 11,000 employees was truly in our hands.

When I called our legal team at Kirkland & Ellis to tell them the news, they weren't too surprised. I guess they had been through enough of these situations to see it coming. They suggested that our CRO take the leadership reins. It had only been a few weeks since we had named John Boken our CRO, so I was obviously hesitant to grant him the top post. I wasn't sure who would be best to take over, but I knew I wasn't going to make the decision lightly.

At first I agreed that John would be a fine choice. I started talking to the executive team and the board of directors. I wanted their input before jumping to any major decisions. I went to every single division head and had a one-on-one conversation. They did not seem too concerned about Phil's departure, but didn't like the idea of someone who had only been with the company a few weeks becoming CEO. I talked to all the division heads in one day. The next day a few of them came to me and asked if I would consider being CEO; others asked why I wasn't considering myself. Though I was reluctant to assume the top post, being reassured by the executive team that they would support me gave me the courage. I went to my most trusted advisor, Chuck, and he agreed it made sense. We both knew it was a huge sacrifice for our family. Our hotel business supported us, and even without Flying J we would be fine. I needed to run the idea by the board, our attorneys, and our bankruptcy team. I was surprised at the support I found from most everyone—especially the employees. People seemed to like having a Call serve as president and CEO and thought that would help restore trust in the company among our creditors and employees. With their blessing, I decided to step into the role of president and CEO.

Honestly it was a dream come true. I had never done something so meaningful and impactful. In another way it was a nightmare. There was so much we needed to overcome. First and foremost we needed to pay creditors back and keep as many jobs as possible. As I sat thinking of all the positive and negative possibilities, e-mails started popping up in my inbox. I was overwhelmed with support and words of encouragement. The big question was, could I walk the walk?

On January 19, 2009, I officially became CEO and president of Flying J. In a month's time I had gone from a stay-at-home mom and board member to the CEO of a major company. A month ago my biggest worry was what to get my kids for Christmas, and now I had no idea how we were going to pull a major company out of Chapter 11. I had a nervous excitement and knew that we—the entire Flying J team, from top management to the employees on the front lines—could do it. But I needed everyone to be on the same page working together to figure out how.

As I stepped into my new role, I knew I needed to determine what kind of leader I was going to be. Whether at home or at the office, I had always maintained that transparency, honesty, and trust would be the foundation of who I was. Honesty, I believed and still believe, is essential to all interactions. If trust between two people doesn't exist, then there is truly no relationship.

Now more than ever I needed to trust those around me, and they needed to trust me. I took this mind-set into all of my meetings, regardless of whom I was working with. Building trust with all the stakeholders was the cornerstone of our successful exit from bankruptcy. I decided my top priority would be to meet with people throughout the company. I wanted to be a transparent leader who listened thoughtfully and carefully to their needs, concerns, and ideas. My dad had hired people he trusted, and then he let them do their jobs. I needed that personal autonomy and confidence restored within each and every employee.

Unfortunately, as I met with more and more Flying J employees, I quickly realized that a culture of fear and intimidation was widespread throughout the company. Employees expressed feeling insecure, judged, and resentful. It wasn't that they lacked knowledge and skills to be effective at their jobs. It was something else. Most had enjoyed working at Flying J because it was a fast-paced, growing company and there was much to be accomplished. The negative was that many did not feel they had been listened to or trusted to do their jobs. Instead they were *told* how to do them.

Many employees felt betrayed. They told me that they had been doing their jobs exactly as they were instructed, and they simply didn't understand how the company could be in this position. How did we, the leaders at the top, let this happen—especially with no warning? I understood why they were angry. Flying J had always been a risk-taking company, but this time we'd gone too far. And it wasn't just going to impact me or our balance sheet; these people, many of whom had worked for decades at the company, were now at risk of losing their jobs. Their livelihoods and their ability to support their families were in question. And here I was, stepping in to try to reposition the company on the right track. They put their hope in me. They believed that I could restore Jay Call's principles and pull the company out of the fire. I wanted to prove them right.

I felt like I was back with my mother visiting Diet Center franchises. I listened to the complaints and hard-luck stories of the employees and reassured them with an apology or a pep talk that things would be better and a promise to do my best. I knew it was important for them to know I was capable of listening to my employees and that I respected their opinions and feelings.

I ultimately decided to hold a whiteboard brainstorming session with all the leaders from Flying J and our subsidiaries. This amounted to about 100 employees from top-level positions. I wanted to know what they thought the company was doing right and what we were doing wrong. I knew that for too long their ideas hadn't been heeded nor their experience valued. Now was an opportunity to put our collective brains together and discover solutions. Together we needed to identify and eliminate waste and problem areas. We spent nearly an entire day fleshing out a range of possibilities. I wanted to hear what was working and what wasn't working. What did they think could be cut? Where could we improve?

Our first elimination was a new driver services program that was about to be rolled out. The program was going to provide back-office and administrative tasks like tax services to drivers. It was easy to see that now wasn't the time to roll out a new service. I crossed it off the whiteboard, and just like that it was gone—and unfortunately so were 40 jobs.

One by one we examined each division and subsidiary. Any program or initiative that was draining resources or deemed too experimental was cut. We also looked at company culture and morale. The dress code was brought up. One employee asked if we could get rid of wearing neckties. Without hesitation I said, "Take them off." It was a simple gesture, but one that went a long way toward showing the brainstorming team and all employees that any idea—no matter how small or seemingly insignificant—would be considered. This was everyone's company. Within a few hours there were no ties left in the building.

Before long there was an energy among the team. We were excited. We could do this. It was tough to decide what to eliminate, especially knowing that someone's job might be on the line, but together we were making progress. I left that day with a surge of energy and motivation, but I knew I needed to keep that momentum going.

Meeting with Creditors

I also needed to meet with our creditors. I wanted to spell out our situation clearly and honestly. Though the meeting overall went well, it was disheartening. The reality was we owed millions, maybe billions of dollars to several organizations. Flying J's problems weren't just ours—they were impacting many companies and the people that worked for them. I received a call one day from one of our small vendors. He only needed a payment from us of a few thousand dollars, but without it he was likely to go bankrupt. He hoped that since it was a small amount that I could pay it. It was so hard to tell him I could not pay any past debt until our case was settled.

Our CRO began the creditors' meeting by explaining how Flying J got into this tight spot and breaking down each problem area. It was clear that our situation was dire, and we needed the creditors' patience and trust if we were going to pull through.

As I listened to the CRO, I was filled with guilt, anger, sadness, and embarrassment. As leader of the company, I knew it was my responsibility to take ownership of the multitude of problems we had caused. As I listened to him break down our issues and debt, I became determined to pay each and every debt back with interest. That was the kind of leader I was going to be—one who stood up to failures, admitted wrongdoings, and paid what we owed. I wasn't going to hide from or ignore our problems—I was going to face them head on.

After the CRO spoke, I stood up to introduce myself. I was a stranger to most of the people in the room, but I didn't let intimidation get the best of me. I needed them to trust me. I did my best to explain who I was and why I was there. Although we were the culprit, Flying J was on their side, I explained.

"We are going to pay you back," I promised—a promise I imagine they thought was empty.

But it wasn't.

I meant it.

Afterward I was surprised by how understanding the group became. A few even thanked me for being so open and honest about our situation. Maybe they felt bad for us. Maybe they believed my promise. Regardless, I left that meeting feeling the same mix of emotions that filled me in the beginning—guilt, anger, sadness, and embarrassment. In a way I felt defeated—a feeling I couldn't allow to linger long.

Saving a Company

Principle: Take on challenges head on with confidence and determination.

My first month as CEO and president was a whirlwind. There were problems to solve no matter which direction I looked in—problems that could have overwhelmed me in no time. I realized that we needed to move quickly. Our choices would affect hundreds of families. I ran from one crisis to another, doing my best to stay positive and productive. There were many troubling talks, sleepless nights, and painful realities that I had to face. But I kept moving forward one day at a time—I had no other choice.

That's not to say that I did it alone. I had many advisors and Flying J executives helping, not to mention my family supporting me in the background and Chuck helping me every step of the way. My essential role was to keep everything moving in the right direction. Chuck was not only a trusted advisor to me in the evenings; he also handled things at home and for Crystal

Inn. There were so many responsibilities that needed immediate attention we became master jugglers. It was my job to focus on one problem and switch to the next problem seamlessly, without ever dropping a ball. I believe my ability to compartmentalize each issue and not worry was essential to my survival those first few weeks and throughout the entire process. I believe that confidence starts when you stop worrying. I would take one problem at a time, one day at a time. I learned at an early age that worrying played no productive role in problem solving. I've seen worry paralyze individuals who had no reason to be so concerned about the future. They worry about the economy, or what people think of them. At some point you have to recognize that worrying won't solve anything—only *you* can solve the problems you're faced with.

Once Flying J's daily cash problems were solved there was little doubt in my mind that the Longhorn Pipeline and Bakersfield Refinery were our primary trouble areas. It was clear that we needed to make significant changes at these subsidiaries right away.

Within only a few days of Flying J filing for bankruptcy, the story spread across the industry and country. So many organizations, especially our competitors, were stunned at the news. The phones started ringing. People and organizations offered their help. Several saw partnership opportunities or wanted to know if an asset were up for sale. Even though nearly every lead would fall through, hearing their interest helped me see there was value in the company. Though we were far from finding a real buyer for either the Bakersfield Refinery or the Longhorn Pipeline, just the sheer interest in a possible acquisition gave us hope that a solution was in our future.

One relationship that had to be mended was with ConocoPhillips. My dad had orchestrated a working partnership with Conoco in 1991. For more than a decade Conoco had been one of Flying J's most trusted partners. In 2002, just before my dad died,

Conoco merged with Phillips. My dad pointed out that there was a change-of-control provision in the CFJ agreement giving us the right to buy back our portion of the partnership and to own ConocoPhillips's part before opening the sale up to an outside party. The ensuing argument between the two partners was still ongoing when my dad died. When it was finally deemed that we had the right to buy back our portion, an appraisal showed the worth to be $240 million. At that point Phil chose not to buy it back. In hindsight that was a huge mistake, since five years later Pilot Flying J paid $700 million to ConocoPhillips for the same share of the CFJ joint venture.

By the time I was running Flying J, our relationship with ConocoPhillips was significantly strained. ConocoPhillips did not like that Phil had sought to keep diesel prices low to attract a greater volume of drivers to the plazas and fueling stations. ConocoPhillips wanted *higher* fuel prices—something Phil never approved of. Trust had been broken and the relationship was weak. But we needed ConocoPhillips on our side now more than ever.

During the weeks prior to Phil's departure, we had met with ConocoPhillips to discuss our immediate needs. They were furious. They believed Phil had been all demands and no compromise—until the bankruptcy, when Flying J needed their help. Despite their anger, they agreed to help us those first few weeks. We gave them a note with a first right to dividend payments from the partnership and the ability to sell off properties if they didn't perform, and they extended credit to us. This was critical to our ability to continue to supply the travel plazas and keep daily cash flow.

But as Phil stepped down and I stepped up, it became even clearer that our relationship with ConocoPhillips needed repair. I gave my speech about who I was and what my intentions were. I tried to stress that we really needed their help going forward. In the beginning they seemed willing to help us.

Times weren't easy during the next few months. ConocoPhillips and Flying J went through many ups and downs as we worked through the bankruptcy. ConocoPhillips could have been extremely instrumental in helping us exit Chapter 11. Instead, the years of strained relations left them with a lack of trust that I could not repair overnight. ConocoPhillips had two executives, Randy Fralix and Kevin Tilley, positioned at Flying J to monitor and assist with the partnership. I spent countless hours with Randy and Kevin. They could see what I was doing every day and they began to gain trust and understand what needed to be done to have a successful partnership. I found them both helpful, but when it came to ConocoPhillips's executive management in Houston, it was harder to work through issues.

I worked hard and stayed focused on solving each problem in the best way possible. I also strived to be transparent and honest at all times. I needed to count on others, and I wanted them to be able to count on me. As I made some headway, people who I had never worked with before began to trust me. They were used to working with Phil and hadn't known what to expect from me. When they realized that I was genuinely trying to work Flying J out of bankruptcy and that I meant what I said, they slowly came around. Their trust and belief in me motivated me further. Before long we were all moving full speed ahead in the same direction.

I was emotionally connected to Flying J. It was my dad's company. There was so much at stake for me, my family, and our legacy, as well as the thousands of employees who worked for us. Yet despite all we had to lose, I felt a sense of challenging excitement. I wanted to do this, and I hoped and believed I *could.*

I couldn't help but wonder what my dad would think. What would he do about the situation we were in? Would he approve of me taking over, or would he want Phil to have remained at the helm? Would he approve of the difficult decisions I had already made and the many hard choices facing me in the coming months?

One night I received a phone call from an old, familiar voice—an employee who had worked at the North Salt Lake Refinery for 40 years. He told me that he believed I was the best person for the job. He told me that my dad once told him that if anything ever happened to Flying J or Phil, his daughter could run the company. His encouraging words brought a smile to my face and the extra boost of confidence I needed.

I was asked many times if I thought Flying J would have been in this position had my dad been alive. It was impossible to know what today might have looked like had he never set foot on that plane in March 2003. This got me wondering about the "what ifs." What if crude prices hadn't dropped so sharply? What if we hadn't experienced a cash crunch and we would have easily been able to pay the crude bill? What if we had received the Bakersfield permit a few years sooner so that it could have been running in a much more productive manner? Maybe the refinery would have been profitable. What if we had only put Longhorn into bankruptcy? Could we have avoided putting Flying J into Chapter 11?

Regardless of all the "what ifs" I could play in my head, we *were* in bankruptcy. I had to remind myself that I didn't have the time or energy to spend thinking about what could have been—I needed to focus on the future and getting us out of this dire situation.

I spent the next months focused on three primary tasks:

1. Finding a debtor-in-possession (DIP) loan to cover immediate cash needs.
2. Aligning with strategic partners.
3. Selling off subsidiaries that were losing money.

I met with our board in early February 2009. I wanted to be certain everyone was on the same page. I explained our strategy, focusing on selling subsidiaries instead of the entire company. The board unanimously agreed that this was the best scenario. Chuck was also granted a position on the board, which was a sigh of relief for me. Chuck and I had always worked well together. We knew each other's strengths and weaknesses. It was a symbiotic partnership at home and on the work front.

The company and our employees were hanging in there, but I could tell stress was high and morale was low. I didn't want fear to spread throughout the company and cause more problems. So I decided to make Presidents' Day a corporate holiday, and sent out an e-mail letting everyone know. Every goodwill gesture mattered.

The only way we could keep everything operating and open to generate the needed daily cash was to pay vendors in advance. Thanks to diligent efforts by our employees, this process was put in place quickly. This worked until there was a three-day weekend with banks closed for three days in a row. Our next cash crunch would hit us on Memorial Day, then another one in early July, and then again in August. August's deadline would be much more severe than the others. In August, bonds worth $30 million were due. We needed a DIP loan to ensure we could pay these bills. A DIP loan is a special kind of financing meant for companies that are financially distressed and in bankruptcy. It is to be used to fund a company's operations as the bankruptcy case runs its course. This loan can be provided by a bank or a company and has repayment priority over existing debt.

I tried to stay positive—I knew we would figure out where to find the loan. Though we were in a tough spot, we had a lot of people and companies rooting for us. I didn't think about the "what if we didn't get it" scenarios. I had to focus on getting the job done. But I knew that if we couldn't pay the bills we would run out of fuel supply, our travel plazas wouldn't be able to run, and we wouldn't be able to pay our employees. We had to work something out.

Word got out that we needed working capital in the coming months. A large national trucking firm expressed interest in working with us. As I spoke to the trucking company's CEO, he presented ideas of how we could work together. We talked about the firm buying half of our transportation assets, as well as fueling at the travel plazas and using TCH cards to purchase fuel. They were excited at the possibility of working with us, and so was I. It was a great initial meeting, but it seemed too good to be true. I hoped something could be worked out and planned another meeting with the trucking firm the following month.

Even Pilot, our longtime competitor, showed interest in a potential partnership. Pilot CEO Jimmy Haslam expressed interest in buying our Retail Division. Unfortunately, we were in a lawsuit with Pilot, which made it difficult to have productive discussions.

It was exciting to start seeing interest in our assets grow throughout the industry. I knew that it was farfetched that these deals would work out, but just the possibility of one of these partnerships forming brought so much hope to our situation. While I was hopeful, I was also doubtful. Years of experience told me that deals like these were often too good to be true.

Securing a DIP loan became one of my top priorities during the next several months. But the economy was in a difficult point in early 2009, and traditional DIP lenders were not offering funds. This left us with few options.

At one point I even traveled to Washington, D.C., to see how and if the federal government could help with our situation. It was the midst of the Great Recession, and the government was providing assistance to many companies and industries struggling to survive. Seeking a government loan was just one more option to try. I met with the Utah delegation, including Representatives Jim Matheson and Rob Bishop, and Senators Orrin Hatch and Bob Bennett. But after several discussions I quickly lost hope that any of these meetings were going to result in a real deal. Senator Bennett offered me direct advice, saying bluntly that I didn't belong in Washington and that he couldn't provide assistance. I appreciated his direct, honest approach, and I agreed with his point of view. Though I was happy to have explored this option, I knew that Flying J wasn't going to receive government assistance.

There were several loan-to-own organizations that our investment bankers at Blackstone had come up with, but their terms were horrible and I couldn't see us working with them. Still, I knew they were there in the background, willing and ready to help us if needed. But accepting their financial help would come at a high price.

It made the most sense that we work with ConocoPhillips, our joint venture partner in CFJ. In many ways, ConocoPhillips wanted us to get back on our feet. They granted us credit only a few days after we filed for bankruptcy. That credit really made a huge difference in our ability to move forward after December 22. But, as I'd soon discover, working out the DIP loan details with ConocoPhillips would prove far more difficult than I anticipated.

ConocoPhillips spent several weeks evaluating our situation, trying to determine whether DIP financing made sense from their perspective. "We're not a bank—this has to make business sense for us," they told me over and over again. I understood and respected the situation they were in.

I spent hours on phone call after phone call and in meeting after meeting trying to work out the details. I began to grow impatient. ConocoPhillips wasn't saying no, but they weren't saying yes either. Regardless of how wishy-washy they were in the beginning, I believed they were ultimately on our side and would provide us with a DIP loan; it was in their best interest to do so. I also knew that creating a DIP loan gave them an opportunity to renegotiate the terms of our original joint venture agreement, which was an opportunity I couldn't see them passing up.

It wasn't until April that we finally met face to face with ConocoPhillips and I was given the opportunity to fully explain our situation and our three-step emergence plan. Everyone seemed on board with our plan, and I left feeling good about where we were in the DIP loan process. Moreover, I was hopeful that we were strengthening our partnership with ConocoPhillips as we worked together to solve this major problem.

I waited anxiously the next several days to hear what they were willing to offer. Finally we received their term sheet. I couldn't believe what I was reading; it was a terrible letdown. ConocoPhillips wanted all of the CFJ joint venture as collateral, and wanted CFJ operations run by a CFJ executive and turned over to them. Their terms were unreasonable and unrealistic, and there was no way this deal was going to happen. It became clear that this was going to be a long, arduous negotiating process.

I spent the next several days fleshing out our ideas for the DIP loan. I wanted to be clear with our needs and expectations, while also being flexible about ConocoPhillips's interests. We met again to discuss the situation. I explained how we needed their help to move forward. I truly believed that our best option was to align with them, and I hoped that they would help. They seemed willing to negotiate and we started working on version two of the DIP loan term sheet. My hopes were high.

A month later we were still in the negotiating process. I spent hours talking with advisors and working through the details. We needed ConocoPhillips, but we also needed to protect ourselves. We received another term sheet, and it was nuts. It was as though they didn't even glance at the changes we had made. Instead they got even stronger on the points that they wanted.

I began to feel defeated. We had worked so hard and were honest with our needs and expectations, yet they were seemingly unwilling to negotiate. I couldn't see a way to save our equity, or for that matter the company. It was approaching mid-May, and we still hadn't reached a compromise. It was becoming harder and harder to see a light at the end of the tunnel.

Moving Forward Without ConocoPhillips?

I was going to have to tell ConocoPhillips no. Our most likely ally was turning into the enemy. We would walk away before we would agree to all they were asking for. The term sheet didn't offer anything that we could really use, and I needed to be able to leave with something of value. Giving up control of the company and getting nothing in return was not acceptable. Our advisors didn't think the creditors would approve the DIP loan, even if the Flying J board did.

I told ConocoPhillips that if we couldn't work something out and we didn't get the DIP loan, the road would be rough, but we would work through it—with or without their help. Moving forward without the DIP loan wouldn't just impact *us*—it would also impact the CFJ joint venture and its operations. ConocoPhillips's interests would also be devalued. Ultimately the decision was up to them. We left with the ball in their court. In the meantime we would be forced to consider other options.

Walking away with nearly nothing accomplished felt horrible. We had all worked so hard and to see nothing come of it was disheartening. I couldn't seal the company's fate by giving in to ConocoPhillips's demands. I expected a fair deal. But the clock was ticking, and we were running out of time.

I learned early on that clear and honest communication was essential throughout our bankruptcy process, including our dealings with ConocoPhillips. We needed to spell out exactly what we expected and needed. But though we had strived to be clear and honest, our communication method was obviously not working with them. We had a great relationship and understanding with the ConocoPhillips executives on the ground, but when they took discussions to the next level in their organization things stalled or got worse.

A few weeks later we met with them again. I had grown more and more pessimistic about our relationship with them and our ability to make this DIP loan happen. But I was happy that we were at the table again trying to work together.

Unfortunately we got off to a rough start. We spent the morning going through commercial terms. As we dug deeper into the agreement it seemed like ConocoPhillips was again demanding more control of CFJ. It was as though nothing had changed, as though they again hadn't read our proposals. I expressed my concerns and they were adamant that taking control was not their intent. They were only trying to protect their assets.

I kept pushing throughout the day. We had proposed a new plan with a traditional corporate structure and a managing board. We agreed that ConocoPhillips would be the operator and subcontract to Flying J.

We made progress, and it began to feel as though the DIP loan may really happen. But it was far from perfect. Our next step was to present the DIP plan to our creditors. We needed them to be assured that we had our cash crunch situation under control.

But again, we weren't on the same page with ConocoPhillips. As we presented our DIP plan to the creditors, it was easy for them to see that our goals weren't aligned, and they didn't like what they saw. Before we knew it, the creditors were making a 180-degree change. Instead of voicing their concerns about our lack of liquidity, they were questioning if we needed the DIP loan that ConocoPhillips had presented. They questioned its size—they thought it was too large, especially considering the cost of the commercial terms. We spent four hours with the group and then another few hours with just the creditors. In the end we got nowhere with ConocoPhillips, but for the first time I felt the creditors were on my side.

It was far past time to find a compromise that worked for both of us. If we couldn't strike a deal it was time to forget about it. We had spent countless hours working on securing a DIP loan. Flying J could not afford to waste more time running in circles.

Our team of FJ executives and advisors, along with representatives from the creditors' committee, debated for hours until we decided to tell ConocoPhillips that the deal wasn't going to happen unless they agreed to our list of expectations. Drawing the line made our advisors nervous, but I knew it was the right move. To date, the DIP terms they proposed offered little financial help with high demands—we couldn't accept them without some compromise. I agreed to call ConocoPhillips and inform them of our decision.

Selling the Longhorn Pipeline

By the end of June we had spent months in a tug-of-war, working back and forth trying to get the deal with ConocoPhillips done. Meanwhile, we worked to sell other assets that would generate enough cash to exit Chapter 11.

When we entered bankruptcy in December 2008, everyone agreed that it was time to put the Longhorn Pipeline on the market. The pipeline had experienced years of ups and downs, and faced its final hurdle in 2008 when oil prices crashed. But there was one major problem hindering its sale: the pipeline was full of more than 900,000 barrels of winter-grade product that had to be sold and moved by April. The winter-grade product would no longer be legal to sell in warmer months, which meant we needed to get the pipeline running again. If we couldn't move the product by spring, the pipeline would be forced to shut down until the fall of 2009, or all the product downgraded—a risk and expense Flying J couldn't afford.

While I and much of the executive team were in the midst of juggling the myriad of issues that came with our bankruptcy—including the DIP loan with ConocoPhillips and the Bakersfield Refinery sale—investment bankers from Blackstone and Aegon, Flying J's supply team, and the Longhorn executives, spearheaded the Longhorn Pipeline divestiture. They were charged with finding a solution to move the winter-grade product out of the pipeline by April, as well as finding a potential buyer for the pipeline.

Their first action was to secure DIP financing to keep the pipeline running. Without the financing we wouldn't be able to resume operations, and the winter-grade product would be forced to sit unused for the rest of the season. By February, just more than a month after our bankruptcy filing, Longhorn was granted a $10 million DIP loan from Merrill Lynch, which was integral to the pipeline's eventual sale. With $10 million financing in place, we began moving the winter-grade product through the pipeline.

The DIP loan couldn't have come at a better time, as more and more buyers were beginning to show interest in acquiring the winter-grade product and sales from the pipeline were profitable, at least for the time being. Buyers across the Southwest and West, who were being slammed by the volatile markets, were looking for product delivery flexibility, which we could afford them. Before we knew it the entire lot of winter-grade product was sold. But we still needed to actually move the product through the pipeline and refill it with summer-grade product, which would incur further costs.

In March 2009, we were granted a $1.5 million DIP financing increase to help us unload the product to its buyers by April. In the meantime we continued searching for a buyer. Fortunately we'd already received a number of bids—one much higher than the rest.

In May we heard from Magellan Midstream Partners, LP, which had shown earnest interest in acquiring Longhorn. Based in Tulsa, Oklahoma, we had a long relationship with Magellan, which specialized in refined petroleum products pipeline systems, and had operated Longhorn since January 2005. We knew that Magellan's potential acquisition was likely to work out, and we focused our efforts toward making the sale happen.

Now that the product was flowing through the pipeline it was beginning to generate a profit, which we knew would greatly help our creditors as well as aid our selling position. We were granted another $20 million revolving loan from Longhorn Pipeline Investors LLC, which had originally sold the Longhorn Pipeline to Flying J in 2006. With the revolving credit line we were able to continue robust operations at Longhorn. Unlike our other assets, the Longhorn Pipeline process was going just about as smoothly as we could have hoped for.

On July 27, 2009, Magellan officially acquired the Longhorn Pipeline in a $350 million deal. The acquisition, which was financed by Magellan, included the Longhorn Pipeline and its remaining product, and a terminal in El Paso that included more than 900,000 barrels of storage. The sale was essential to moving Flying J one step closer to emerging from Chapter 11 bankruptcy and was a much-needed triumph. The team involved in this transaction performed a miracle by keeping a large sale price firm.

Challenges with the Bakersfield Refinery

It was now evident that acquiring the Bakersfield Refinery had proven to be a huge mistake. We had already invested hundreds of millions of dollars into enhancing and improving the refinery's outdated infrastructure. Unfortunately, it was clear that we would likely never see a return on those millions of dollars invested. It was painful, but a part of our new reality.

As we worked toward solving our cash-crunch problems, one of the first steps we took was determining which assets we needed to divest immediately. We decided to search for buyers for the Bakersfield Refinery. As the company stepped into Chapter 11, Phil and I had agreed that Bakersfield needed to cease refining crude oil. One of the decisions made in the earliest days of our bankruptcy was to close Bakersfield down for 10 days for a maintenance and safety check. We quickly realized that we didn't have the cash needed to continue purchasing crude oil and running the refinery. With no ability to buy crude or finish the upgrade, Bakersfield was put on the market for sale. Under our ownership, the refinery never fully resumed operations. The cost to keep it warm or running at a minimal capacity so we could sell it came with a price tag of $3 million per month. But we didn't have a choice—keeping it warm even though it was not processing crude oil was important in order to keep certain operating permits active until a buyer could be found. So we opted to operate it as minimally as possible and work toward finding a potential buyer. We notified our employees at the Bakersfield Refinery that we would begin shutting the refinery down and that it would be mostly closed, except for minimal operations, within 60 days. The refinery employed hundreds of hardworking people who would lose their jobs in a time when finding new employment was next to impossible. Their lives were going to change, and it was because of our situation. This was our first significant employee loss. It was horrible. We needed a sale to happen soon.

Even though we were shutting down and searching for a buyer, the State of California still wanted to keep the refinery up and running. I participated in calls with government officials that I never would have envisioned having a dialog with, such as

California governor Pete Wilson. He wanted to know how the state could help to keep Bakersfield operating. The Bakersfield Refinery supplied 6 percent of the diesel fuel and 2 percent of the gasoline in California, which the state desperately needed. The governor said the state would try to help us get more access to crude oil, and he also thought the state would be able to put pressure on banks to send TARP (Troubled Asset Relief Program) money our way. Given the problems the State of California was having, I knew this was not likely to happen, but it was a nice gesture by the governor.

Meanwhile, potential buyers were beginning to express interest in the Bakersfield Refinery, but it wasn't going to be a simple process. Industry analysts said an acquisition would be difficult in light of the country's lower demand for fuel.

Our investment bank, Deutsche Bank, painted a doom-and-gloom picture for our prospects. They believed the refinery could not sell based on just the equipment upgrade and permits. Still, Deutsche Bank was moving ahead on selling it. In addition, during the first weeks of the bankruptcy I had met with International Alliance Group, an engineering firm that was helping us sell the uninstalled Bakersfield equipment. IAG had assured me they could sell our equipment for cost. We thought we may get as much as $60 million cash for this upgraded equipment, which would have been much-needed cash if we could have sold it. However, after nearly two months IAG had no takers for the equipment. We held firm on our plans to sell Bakersfield and began receiving bids.

One of the biggest issues we faced as we marketed the Bakersfield Refinery was that most organizations that showed interest in acquiring it really wanted a package deal that also included the North Salt Lake Refinery. North Salt Lake was a crown jewel in the refinery world, so we weren't eager to include it in a package deal with Bakersfield. I decided to hold firm that North Salt Lake wasn't for sale, but the reality was that I knew in order to keep the travel plaza business it may be necessary to sell the North Salt Lake Refinery as well. Although I knew it was not wise to officially put the North Salt Lake Refinery on the auction block, we would entertain meetings with interested parties. I knew it was wiser to keep all options open, regardless of how unattractive they were at the time.

The first organization to show real interest in acquiring the Bakersfield Refinery was Red Leaf Resources. Red Leaf was a Utah-based startup developing oil shale technology. They believed Bakersfield might be the perfect fit for their oil-refining needs. More importantly, they were excited about the potential—almost too excited. Still, we talked about developing a joint venture that would be mutually beneficial. By the end of our discussions I'd become more and more skeptical. I told them to review everything carefully and make us an offer.

We also had many lowball offers come out of the woodwork, but I knew they weren't realistic options. Still, I was happy to see interest growing. In the meantime, we had to start working through union negotiations at Bakersfield.

After we met with Red Leaf Resources, our next serious meeting was with EOR Energy Services, a Houston-based diversified energy company with a focus on the oil and gas industry. They outlined a conceptual offer for the Bakersfield Refinery, the North Salt Lake Refinery, and Flying J Oil and Gas, which offered oil and gas exploration and production services, along with possibly including the Longhorn Pipeline. They laid out a partnership offer in which we had 60 percent ownership until the upgrade at Bakersfield was complete, and then 40 percent after the upgrade. They also presented a second deal, which included $1 billion to buy the refineries outright.

We were all intrigued with EOR's offers. At first I leaned toward the partnership because we would have more ability to keep employees happy. But as I closely examined it and weighed the risks involved, I realized that it was better to try to do an outright sale to EOR.

If we could get close to that, we would be able to pay creditors 100 percent of what we owed. We would also leave Flying J in a lot better position, with little or no debt and the retail chain intact. But the big questions remained: Where is the money? Can these guys really come through with a cash offer?

Glencore, an international commodities company with a focus on energy products, was another company that showed real interest in acquiring the refinery. Glencore proposed buying the Longhorn Pipeline, Bakersfield Refinery, and North Salt Lake Refinery in a package deal that would keep Flying J on as a partner. But again, it seemed too good to be true. It was another one of those companies that seemed to be offering us the world.

By May 2009 the selling process was moving slowly but steadily. We received a few Bakersfield Refinery bids that seemed promising and real. The bids were around $50 million to $60 million, but none included financing or purchase agreements so they were a bit sketchy as offers go. One company that had showed interest in the past, Alon USA Energy, quickly became the most qualified bidder. Once we let them know they were our first choice they began to drag their feet on a closing date. Meanwhile, most other interested parties disappeared as we pressured Alon. Most of these deals really had been to good to be true, and we knew we would be lucky to keep Alon interested.

Flying J Oil and Gas

Beyond the Bakersfield Refinery and Longhorn Pipeline, we decided to divest our noncore assets. One of our smaller entities was Flying J Oil and Gas, headquartered in North Salt Lake since 1980. The exploration unit focused its development activities in the

Intermountain West and had core operations in the Uinta Basin in eastern Utah and the Williston Basin in eastern Montana, with an interest in around 200 gas and oil wells.

I didn't want to sell Oil and Gas, as it was profitable, but the creditors' committee pressured us to put this company up for auction. In fact, it was the *only* profitable asset that we immediately put up for sale using the bankruptcy auction process. Though I was opposed to selling it, I did it as a gesture of goodwill for the creditors' committee so that they'd understand I was serious about paying them back.

By the end of 2009 there were two companies bidding for the opportunity to acquire Oil and Gas: El Paso E&P Company and Citation Oil & Gas Corp. Both were great potential buyers that were willing to meet our expedited closing date of December 31, 2009.

Citation, a Houston-based oil and gas acquisition, development, and production company, put in the highest bid at $92 million, which we were prepared to accept. But while literally waiting in bankruptcy court seeking approval to sell Oil and Gas to Citation, El Paso, another oil and gas company headquartered in Houston, put in a last-minute bid. The court granted us a short recess to review El Paso's offer. As if it were being played out in a drama on television, our team of investment bankers and executives spent the next three hours in a bidding war that took place in the hallways outside the courtroom until El Paso finally won the rights to acquire Oil and Gas for $103.5 million. The deal was finalized on December 29, 2009. Again, I can take little credit for this very successful transaction that was led by our exploration and production counsel, Chris Malan, and our investment banker, Blackstone.

Since 1997, Flying J Insurance Services had provided insurance to the trucking industry. By the time of the bankruptcy it was placing approximately $25 million in insurance premiums annually. In our efforts to raise cash and show our creditors how committed we were to paying them back, this was another subsidiary put on the market. The president of Flying J Insurance, Mark Farmer, culminated this sale with Utah-based The Buckner Company, which agreed to acquire it effective January 1, 2010.

Flying J also owned a small petroleum jobber based in North Salt Lake called Haycock Petroleum. Haycock wasn't profitable and bordered on bankruptcy because of Flying J's inability to help with credit in the slow months. Because it was a nonessential asset, it made sense to try to find a buyer. Chuck agreed to lead this process along with current management. Haycock received marginal interest from prospective buyers, which primarily wanted to acquire Haycock in a package deal with other assets. None of the bids we received looked particularly promising, but we kept at it, knowing that eventually a bidder with the right price and attributes would come through.

By summer's end we finally had a potential buyer that was serious about acquiring Haycock. Texas-based C. L. Thomas signed the deal to acquire it on September 4, 2009. The deal, which included 16 warehouses and cardlock facilities in Utah, Nevada, Idaho, and California, was finalized by October 1.

The Best Option

Principle: Negotiating in good faith, trust, and open communication lead to mutually beneficial deals.

Rumors grew quickly after the Flying J bankruptcy announcement. Everyone, including our competitors, our vendors, and our partners, wanted to know exactly what had happened and what we were doing to get out of it. Additionally, nearly everyone seemed to have their own theory of what our situation was. Brushing off the rumors didn't come easily to me, but I knew it came with the territory. It was my job to reassure everyone we dealt with that we were digging ourselves out of this mess and it was under control, despite the rumors claiming otherwise.

Rumors weren't the only things swirling around us. I heard numerous "solutions" to our situation. I guess the answers to our problems seemed easy to some—though that was far from *our* reality.

Most of the ideas came with a catch that included the sale of one or more of our core businesses to the entity proposing the idea. At first I entertained some of these proposals, but in most cases I found out quickly they were too good to be true.

Jimmy Haslam, CEO of Pilot Corporation, was one of many who wanted to meet with me to discuss Flying J's bankruptcy. Pilot had been a longtime Flying J competitor, with whom we were currently engaged in an antitrust lawsuit over alleged price-fixing brought by Flying J. Ironically, Pilot's origin and vision were similar to Flying J's. Pilot was founded by Jim Haslam in 1958 and grew to become one of the nation's largest petroleum and truck stop companies by the early 1990s. Jim's son, Jimmy Haslam, had been president and CEO since 1996.

Though we were competitors, Phil and Jimmy had met in the late 1990s to discuss merging the two companies. And in 2003, after my dad's death, Jimmy flew to Salt Lake and met with Thad and me to again talk about a possible merger. Both times early discussions ended and the companies continued down different paths. While Pilot pursued large fleets with smaller facilities, Flying J continued to build large facilities focusing on building loyalty with the owner/operator by offering a low street price and many services to help them manage their small businesses. Like most competitors, both companies believed they were far better than the other. We were fierce competitors over the years, often building facilities off the same interstate exits to compete head to head.

As Flying J began to climb out of Chapter 11 in 2009, and as the rumors of our circumstances continued to grow around us, I heard over and over again that Pilot was planning to buy out Flying J—rumors that made my blood boil. After filing bankruptcy, we had never seriously considered merging with or selling assets to Pilot. Yet the rumors had spread even to our employees. It was frustrating, and it drove me crazy.

During those first few months, Jimmy called and wanted to meet. When he first called I was advised not to meet because of our pending lawsuit. Moreover, because of the rumors I was telling people almost daily that we were not selling to Pilot, so I was concerned that if I met with Jimmy and we struck a deal I would appear dishonest. The rumors had gone too far, and they were just another reason I chose to stay clear of Jimmy during those early months. But Jimmy was persistent. He kept calling requesting a meeting. Often in those calls, Jimmy expressed interest in partnering with Flying J or buying the company. I would politely decline and tell him that because of the lawsuit and rumors it did not make sense to further our discussions. Jimmy was always a gentleman on the calls and even agreed to try to stop his sales team from spreading rumors.

Jimmy called again in late May 2009. He was flying to the West Coast to attend a wedding. He asked if he could make a stop in Salt Lake so the two of us could at least meet. Though I had put him off for months I knew that I couldn't let pride stop me from leaving this option open. I decided why not, what harm could come from it? He had been persistent over the last few months, so he was obviously interested in our situation, and he had been able to calm the rumors. I decided to hear him out. In June, Jimmy landed in Salt Lake and we had a nice, get-better-acquainted discussion before I launched into my ideas about settling the antitrust lawsuit. Jimmy wasn't interested in discussing our pending lawsuit at all. He was in town for another reason—he wanted to talk about how Flying J and Pilot could partner together.

I had met with many people who thought they had the solution to our problems, but no one had been able to offer a real get-down-to-work solution. I thought my meeting with Jimmy would be just like the others. He'd offer his big ideas about what we should do, and I'd listen politely knowing that his plans likely wouldn't work. But as I stepped into the Metropolitan restaurant in downtown Salt Lake that early summer day, I was ready and willing to hear him out. I wanted to find a solution and wasn't going to close my mind to his suggestions simply because Pilot was a competitor.

Jimmy was a true southern gentleman. He was kind, warm, and listened with intensity. He wasn't there to push his ideas or agenda—he seemed to truly care about our situation. It was as though he was a kindred spirit with me and Flying J; after all, both companies were started by our fathers, and both eventually ended up in our hands. Of course Jimmy's drive to help us emerge from Chapter 11 was ultimately a business decision that would prop up Pilot. But more than strictly business, Jimmy projected a sense of genuineness that I found unique and refreshing. He was unlike the many others we had worked with throughout our situation during the past tumultuous months.

Jimmy started his straightforward and simple pitch by saying, "Our companies could be amazing together and let me tell you why." He began writing his plans on a paper tablecloth that covered our table. As I watched his plans unfold, I could feel myself growing excited. He had a plan that at first glance seemed to be a win-win for both organizations. He explained that he wanted to acquire our truck plazas. We brainstormed together for three hours and came up with a plan and numbers sketched out on that paper table-cloth. We would merge the two companies, including the North Salt Lake Refinery. He would pay us the cash Flying J needed to emerge from bankruptcy and we would use any remaining value as equity in the merged company. Although he was not familiar with DIP loans, he was not opposed to considering helping us with that as well.

It seemed like we had a very workable solution. If we received at least $400 million cash, we could emerge from bankruptcy and pay everyone back 100 percent of what we owed them. His ideas made sense, but what impressed me most was what he had to say about how the future business would operate. It was clear he understood our industry and had a vision for what our two companies could be together.

An attractive part of the merger proposal was that the Flying J brand would remain active. Jimmy recognized the value of the brand and reassured me that he would not rebrand our travel plazas to be Pilot stores. Instead he would find a way to create a complementary strategy. Being able to keep the Flying J brand and equity in the merged company was the best alternative I had found.

The negative aspects of the proposal were that we'd have to downsize our Ogden headquarters and Pilot would assume operations of our travel plazas, neither of which would be easy. Maybe this was the solution.

Jimmy confidently spoke about how our organizations could work seamlessly together. It was clear that he was a great operator, and integration under his direction had the best chance for success. His confidence in his ability to see this through, regardless of how difficult it would be, gave me hope for a bright future for the Flying J brand. He was willing to listen to our needs and expectations, roll up his sleeves, and get this done.

By the end of our meeting I was convinced that this was it—this was the plan we needed to move forward. If our tablecloth plan could come together, we could likely emerge out of bankruptcy quite quickly and pay everyone back what they were owed. The best part was the growing confidence I felt in Jimmy's ability to build an amazing company out of two brands. Finally, after months of nonstop, strenuous work, I finally had a glimpse of a light at the end of the tunnel.

Could It Really Work?

I left our long lunch feeling elated. Maybe I should have been apprehensive. But my gut told me that this could work. Merging our truck stops and travel plazas with Pilot's could be the way out of Chapter 11.

I drove to Park City, where I was meeting with Chuck and my mom. As I drove up the canyon, all I could think of were the possibilities that were ahead of us. With $400 million we would be able to emerge from bankruptcy and pay back every single creditor with interest. We would still have an ownership stake in the new company and the Flying J brand would continue. We would be back on track by the end of summer, and then we could focus on rebuilding the company and moving it forward. I was excited.

I sat down at the table with Chuck and my mom. I'm sure I was beaming and smiling from ear to ear. "I have a deal with Pilot that I think will work," I exclaimed.

As I explained the details, Chuck and my mom were supportive. They could see that Jimmy's plan was a reasonable offer that could prove to be a mutually beneficial solution. Though I'm sure they were a bit skeptical that everything would work out perfectly, I could sense their excitement growing too.

First thing the next morning, I called Flying J's investment banker and spelled out Jimmy's plan. He thought I was crazy and that the deal would never go through. He said it didn't make sense that someone like Jimmy would offer to do all of these things for us, including the DIP loan. He said it simply wasn't in Pilot's best interest and that "the deal would get done when pigs fly." But after my long lunch with Jimmy, I believed in his business sense and ideas. Jimmy wasn't just interested in a merger; he was dedicated to making it work. He was committed to the long-term value.

Next I called our attorney, who also agreed that the deal sounded too good to be true. But it was his and our investment banker's jobs to be skeptical, especially when it came to a deal of this magnitude and in an economic environment like it was during the summer of 2009. Their pessimism only gave me more incentive to get the deal done.

I also heard from Jimmy that day. He had already spoken with his executive team, and they were on board. He even felt confident that the DIP loan would happen. We drafted up a term sheet and the ball was officially in motion.

At that point I had been CEO at Flying J for more than six months and knew we had opportunities to improve our profit beyond what our current income statement reflected. For instance, we ran our restaurants at a loss. I believed we could lease the restaurant space out to restaurant organizations at all of our plazas and make that department profitable. At the time, we were also refusing to accept Comdata fuel cards, the primary means of payment for many truckers on the road. Coming to an agreement to accept these cards could also add value to our plazas.

Getting many of these tasks done in bankruptcy and with ConocoPhillips as a partner was nearly impossible. Jimmy was willing to give us value in his offer for some of these items because he agreed they would eventually add to our bottom line. Our team ran numbers to support our ideas for adding value, and we presented our offer to Jimmy.

In the beginning we had talked about selling all of Flying J, which would have included the North Salt Lake Refinery. It also meant our ownership in the merged company would have been closer to 50 percent. After careful analysis, we believed we could keep the refinery if we could refinance our debt.

At our second meeting I was planning on telling Jimmy the refinery was off the table. But it turned out to be a nonissue; Jimmy had decided they did not want ownership in the refinery. However, in addition to Flying J, Pilot wanted to purchase half of our card processing company, TCH.

Our next meeting included Chuck and our Retail Division VP in a hotel meeting room with Jimmy, who used a whiteboard to show us his plan. Jimmy came prepared to talk extensively about the deal, which we did for the next five hours. During our meeting we worked through each aspect of the merger. Jimmy listened and agreed with our arguments for a higher price than our current profitability would justify. We were hoping for a valuation of $1.3 billion, but based on our current EBITDA and EBITDA multiples we would be lucky to get to $1 billion. We all left the meeting feeling optimistic about our future partnership, as well as acknowledging three primary hurdles: the FTC, valuation, and our employees.

At the end of that third meeting, Jimmy was prepared to offer us substantial ownership rights—as much as we could afford. He also afforded us with the opportunity to buy back shares with any leftover cash. Moreover, Pilot was prepared to offer us the much-needed DIP loan.

It was full speed ahead the next few weeks, and by June 26, Jimmy and Pilot had an official offer on the table. The offer included $400 million cash and a 20 percent ownership stake in the company.

I wasn't naïve and knew there would be complications along the way. Merging with Pilot would present several complex issues that we would need to work through. I was especially worried about our employees. I knew that the jobs of a number of employees at our Ogden headquarters, many of whom had been extremely devoted to Flying J for decades, would be in jeopardy. It was heartbreaking to know that so many talented and dedicated people would be negatively impacted, but we didn't have much choice. It was the reality we were facing. I wanted to be certain they were impacted as little as possible.

Another concern that we'd be facing was a possible battle with the Federal Trade Commission. Merging these two giant companies wouldn't be possible without passing painstakingly thorough antitrust tests from the FTC. Little did I know at the time that our battle with the FTC would extend months after Jimmy and I reached an official agreement.

Negotiations during the following months went as smoothly as I could have hoped for. Jimmy and I worked well together. We listened to each other and tried to be fair in our dealings. My father had always taught me that a good deal is when both parties walk away happy. Even though I would have preferred not to merge, given our situation this outcome was about as good as I could have expected. I was happy with it. Jimmy was also extremely happy, because he knew the two companies together had great profit potential. It was the best solution for both of our companies.

Pilot's DIP Loan Offer

Even though the Pilot deal was moving forward, it was not fast enough to solve our issue with $30 million in bonds coming due in early August. Once the deadline hit, the bonds could be called in at any point, and we were nowhere close to having $30 million in cash to cover them. Although we had already sold off the Longhorn Pipeline and Flying J Oil and Gas, those funds were tied up in the bankruptcy and therefore inaccessible. We needed a DIP loan to get through the next several weeks. Without the DIP loan we would be facing another financial crisis—one that would mean we'd again be unable to pay our bills.

For several months we had been working hard with ConocoPhillips to secure the DIP loan, but our negotiations had stalled. They wanted too many concessions, and we weren't going to give in to their demands—no matter how desperate we became. The biggest obstacle was that the DIP loan put the CFJ joint venture largely under ConocoPhillips's control. Regardless of our strong partnership with them and the supposedly forthcoming DIP loan they were to provide us, I knew it was time to move forward with Plan B and finalize Pilot's offer of a DIP loan. Our pending deal with Pilot caught ConocoPhillips off guard, and with the bonds coming due in just weeks, we didn't have the option to continue the back-and-forth negotiating process with them that had proven unsuccessful for months.

Since Jimmy had mentioned that Pilot might be willing to provide the loan with our merger package, it was clear that adding a DIP loan to the process might be the best solution. Jimmy agreed. He was on board without hesitation, and Pilot began drafting a letter of intent. By the first week of July we had a solid Plan B. Meanwhile, the ConocoPhillips DIP loan, our Plan A, was still in the works. Since we had spent so much time with ConocoPhillips, we wanted to see it through, if at all possible. We decided to move forward with the ConocoPhillips DIP loan and replace it with Pilot's if we couldn't reach terms that made sense.

Within a week we were moving forward with both DIP loans. I was up front with ConocoPhillips and kept them in the loop regarding our plans, but they weren't happy—and not just with our prospects of utilizing a DIP loan from Pilot. Our potential merger with Pilot infuriated ConocoPhillips. If the merger were finalized, they would be partners with Pilot instead of Flying J. ConocoPhillips was upset we had not partnered with them to do the deal with Pilot for the whole company, but knowing how difficult ConocoPhillips had been to deal with, I did not have the time to bring them into the deal with Flying J and Pilot. I knew Jimmy would have a better chance negotiating with them separately from us.

Our energy and negotiations were focused toward our pending Pilot deal. Randy and Kevin, the ConocoPhillips representatives who were close to me, completely understood why I had struck a deal with Pilot without their participation, but those higher up in the organization were not pleased. Based on my previous experience working with ConocoPhillips, I knew that if I had included them in the initial Pilot deal, forcing Jimmy to negotiate with all of us, the situation would have stalled and even possibly failed. Creating a separate deal between ConocoPhillips and Pilot was tougher on Jimmy, as he now had two parties to negotiate with. But it also allowed Flying J to be much more nimble and faster with our negotiations, which is what we needed to stay afloat during this tumultuous time.

The biggest risk was that ConocoPhillips would exercise its right of first refusal and try to fight Pilot's merger proposal. Luckily our deal had lots of pieces and would have been hard for ConocoPhillips to take on, but that option still existed. I had numerous phone calls and meetings trying to calm ConocoPhillips's nerves and get the ball rolling with discussions with Pilot.

But ConocoPhillips remained nervous. They owned a 40 percent share in the travel plazas, which meant they could potentially be hugely impacted by Pilot's acquisition of our 60 percent share. I understood their position. We had long been partners and they felt we were undercutting them from the deal. We, on the other hand, didn't have much of a choice. We were in a sticky situation and ConocoPhillips wasn't bending over backward to help us get out of it; we couldn't even reach an agreement with them on the DIP loan, or on simple operating improvements such as leasing restaurants or accepting Comdata fuel cards. Still, I appreciated ConocoPhillips as a longtime partner and wanted to ensure them that this deal didn't negatively impact them. I tried to reassure them that I would do whatever I could to ensure they didn't get the raw end of the deal. I wanted them to be happy with the ultimate outcome. It took some time, but ConocoPhillips eventually saw that our merger with Pilot could benefit them, and they ended up in a very lucrative position.

EBITDA Hurdles

The plan with Pilot was moving forward steadily with no major changes. We were working toward a $1.3 billion offer, to include $400 million cash and a 19 to 22 percent ownership stake for Flying J left in the plazas.

On July 8 we hit our first real snag with the Pilot merger. Some of Jimmy's partners were balking at his $1.3 billion offer. They believed he could acquire our travel plazas for under $1 billion. I grew nervous. I knew Jimmy was a man of his word and would stick to his commitments of a $1.3 billion price, but I couldn't help feel a sense of doubt. We needed this deal to go through as planned knowing the price was at jeopardy of dropping below $1 billion.

It was up to me and our team to convince the Pilot team to accept the higher price. I began gathering all the documentation I could in order to prove our value. Unfortunately, as we were analyzing the numbers and trying to build a case for why we should use the higher price, I learned that we had double-counted some numbers, which was a huge blow to our efforts. I needed every piece of data to justify that our value was higher than our current numbers reflected. Fortunately, I still had Jimmy on my side. Knowing that our future margins could be substantial, he wanted the deal to go through, even if it meant paying a higher price.

Within a day Pilot returned with a lower offer. After examining our numbers they felt this was the total amount they could justify. We were not in the best position to negotiate a higher price. Time was running out because of the tie-in with the DIP loan and our pending bond repayment due in only a few weeks. We needed to agree on a price and deal structure.

We again counter-offered with our $1.3 billion price. We were confident that Pilot was getting a fair deal with our proposed offer. Jimmy agreed with our projections and verbally committed to a higher price, but not as much as we'd proposed. We just needed to be patient, he assured me, suggesting that with time he could work our price up. But all I could think of was our desperate need to file the DIP loan with the bankruptcy court.

Meanwhile, we announced the Pilot deal to our creditors, and their reactions were positive. They quickly recognized how the deal would benefit them, assuming it went through as planned. If the Pilot deal went through, we would reach my goal of paying each and every creditor off fully and with interest. They were unanimously on board.

On July 10, Pilot's team came back with a new figure that was lower than our number. Again Jimmy assured me that he could increase the number if I could give him a few more days. We both knew that I couldn't wait that long—we needed to file with the bankruptcy court that day. The process it would take to get all the necessary approvals in order to have the DIP loan in place by the day the bonds were due was crucial. It was a strict process because of the bankruptcy, and we needed to get started as soon as possible.

Our team's nerves and patience were wearing thin. They worried I was being too aggressive and they didn't want to see the deal fall through. I agreed to the lower price of $1.19 billion, and I asked Jimmy for a commitment that if I agreed to that price Pilot would keep the price firm and not come back with reductions after the due diligence period. I was aware that in many negotiations it was easy to agree to a price, but then one party could justify why something wasn't represented correctly and question the original price. Jimmy readily committed to keep the price firm because he knew what the value of the merged companies together would be. Moreover, he knew he was getting a fantastic deal.

Agreeing to a deal meant that the Pilot DIP loan could move forward. We were now able to repay our bonds with our own cash flow plus $7 million from the DIP loan, which we repaid within only a few days. This was after months of worrying about how we would make these payments or get a DIP loan to fund them. It's likely that we would have been able to make the payment ourselves with no assistance, but it was nice to know that we had the DIP loan in place if needed.

Though everything wasn't lining up exactly as planned, we were moving forward in a positive direction that we all could live with.

A Bittersweet Moment

On July 11, 2009, we filed the signed Pilot/Flying J letter of intent with the court and the creditors' committee. The merger deal points were formally in place. After the signing, Chuck and I boarded the company's large Cessna Sovereign jet for the very last time to meet the extended Haslam family in Tennessee and then sell the plane to the Smucker family. We knew that this deal was the end of a chapter in the history of Flying J. It was ironic that we flew in the same plane that had originally been purchased because it was large enough to make transatlantic flights, since we were once planning to build travel plazas in Europe. Now the Sovereign was being sold and everything had drastically changed.

Chuck and I stayed at Jimmy Haslam's home in Knoxville, Tennessee. Over dinner, Jimmy told us a story of the Haslam kids playing soccer when they were young. Jimmy would tell the kids, "Pretend you are playing Flying J." That's how competitive their family was towards Flying J.

Chuck and Crystal on their way to Knoxville, July 2009.

Negotiating the merger and all the different details of the deal under the circumstances we faced will likely be the most challenging deal I complete in my career. I hope to do many other deals, but not under the shadow of bankruptcy. Even though it was tough, it was exciting and rewarding because I believed the outcome would be positive. There was so much riding on this agreement. Completing the deal would impact many individuals and businesses because it would mean they would be paid back what we owed them. I really would rather have kept the travel plazas, but I wanted to do what was right by our creditors as we emerged from bankruptcy, which meant making tough decisions like selling the travel plaza business. But since we had to sell, I don't think there could have been any better partner than the Haslam family and Pilot. Jimmy went above and beyond his duty to ensure the deal was mutually beneficial. In the end the Flying J brand was preserved, we would remain part owners, most employees would keep their jobs, and creditors would be repaid. Under the circumstances it was the best deal imaginable.

There was still one big hurdle standing in our way to completing the merger with Pilot: the Federal Trade Commission. Before we could sign the papers with Pilot making the merger official, the FTC would scrutinize every minute detail of our plan. Their job was to ensure antitrust compliance and protect consumer interests. Jimmy became obsessed with the case, following every action or inaction that took place. He called his attorneys daily and checked in with me frequently. Neither of us had ever been involved in an investigation of this magnitude and didn't know what to expect. My legal team believed that we could be headed toward a battle, while Jimmy's team initially was far more optimistic.

The Pieces Come Together

Principle: Patience often pays off.

The FTC Weighs In

The Pilot and Flying J executive teams met with the FTC on August 19, 2009. As we stepped into the room filled with 15 or so government employees, I grew nervous. I knew that we had our ducks in a row, but so much was riding on the FTC how could I not feel anxious?

Jimmy and I both explained why our companies should merge. We argued that although we owned two of the country's largest truck stop networks, our merger would combine only 500 of the nation's 5,000 truck stops. Furthermore, we described how Flying J's primary customer base comprised owner/operators and small fleets, while Pilot's customers were large national trucking companies. We went through our presentation, discussing each minuscule detail of what the Pilot and Flying J merger could mean to the industry and customers. As we went through our plans, I could sense excitement growing between our two teams. Our argument made sense to us, but would it make sense to the FTC staff?

The FTC's response wasn't as optimistic. They told us our customers were concerned. For example, they said a customer had expressed concern that while Flying J had been a low-cost fuel provider on the highway, offering low prices to everyone, Pilot had typically offered high-volume discounts to only select customers. They wanted to know how the merger would affect Flying J's popular pricing strategy. At that point we hadn't planned to change the pricing strategy, so customers wouldn't feel an impact, we explained.

As the meeting came to a close, the FTC informed us that they were going to look into our merger agreement a second time before finalizing their decision. They needed to ensure that the deal made sense for both our companies, our competitors, and our customers. Jimmy and I had an idea of who might have talked to the FTC; it was our belief it was not our customers but our *competitors* who didn't want the merger to happen, or at least they would want the right to buy any stores we were selling. It was clear after our meeting the FTC would delay our merger to dig deeper into our two companies and our market share. I was worried that the process would take even longer.

We left the room deflated. The FTC's reaction was depressing and it was very different from what we had hoped. Our attorneys thought we might have to sell a few travel plazas, but what the

FTC told us seemed more like an all-or-nothing proposition. They had not even brought up the possibility of divesting some travel plazas. They mostly spoke of the dominance we would have in the market if we joined together, which we knew wasn't true—500 truck stops out of 5,000 was hardly market dominance.

Our attorneys remained confident that the FTC wouldn't win in court, but we all found their response disturbing. Our next step was to illustrate that customers were buying from many of the independent chains. We needed to show that several fueling options existed and market share was spread among all of them. Even if the Pilot and Flying J merger was approved, there would still be plenty of competition because of the large number of independent chains. Jimmy and I spent many hours discussing possible outcomes. Everything we discussed was mostly speculative because the decision of how we progressed really was in the hands of the FTC. It became a waiting game.

During the next several weeks the FTC was moving slow and steady, and Jimmy and I, but especially Jimmy, were growing more anxious and impatient. He was not used to waiting to get a deal like this done. Once a deal had been reached he expected expediency to closure. Yet weeks were going by with little to no communication from the FTC. At the end of October the FTC informed us that they wanted another 60 days to continue their review process. The new deadline meant the deal, assuming it went through, wouldn't be finalized until mid-January 2010.

The FTC's delay, however, wasn't necessarily a bad thing for Flying J. Though we were anxious to make the merger final and move forward, all of the cash our businesses accumulated throughout the process went directly to Flying J, not Pilot.

The creditors were patiently waiting and happy with the pending outcome, and we were able to focus on our business while we waited. So although I wasn't happy about the delay, because I wanted to pay everyone off and move on, I knew that in some ways it worked to our advantage.

By Thanksgiving we faced more setbacks with the FTC. They were claiming that our data wasn't in compliance, and thus our 60 days may not have started. Despite the FTC setbacks, Pilot was ready to move forward with the deal. Moreover, they had their post-merger plans already in place.

Pilot had become very familiar with our operations over the past few months, and I was getting uncomfortable that if the deal did not go through they may know *too* much. It was time to sign the deal and wait for the FTC. We needed to get back to business.

On December 3, 2009, I flew to Knoxville for a ceremonial signing. Pilot and Flying J had agreed to all the terms of our merger and now we were just waiting for the FTC approval to close the transaction. Jimmy's entire family and several employees were there. I had traveled alone, so there was no one except me from the Call family. As I met Jimmy's father, Pilot founder Jim Haslam Sr., I couldn't help but think of my dad. I believe he would have liked the Haslams

Jimmy and Jim Haslam Sr. and Crystal signing the Pilot Flying J deal on December 3, 2009.

and been happy with the deal we had struck. That was the kind of deal he liked—good for both parties.

Even though the signing was purely ceremonial at the time, I felt a sense of pride as I added my signature. So many events had led us to that moment—especially during the past year. In the end, I wasn't as sad as I thought I would be. I was happy to see our family business going into the hands of another family business. Jimmy was committed to make what he wanted to call Pilot Flying J (PFJ) an amazing success, and we would still be involved as minority owners. In the meantime, while we waited for the FTC's opinion, I had other business transactions to complete in order to solidify a successful exit from bankruptcy.

Right before my next meeting with the FTC, in which I was scheduled for a deposition, I was thrown a curve. I knew Flying J and the Pilot deal inside and out. But the night before the deposition I learned that the FTC had my personal journal. Only then did I remember that my journal was on my laptop, which had been subpoenaed with all our company records. I had been very candid in my writings. I included many of my thoughts, worries, and concerns during the past year. I had nothing to hide, but I questioned whether they would interpret everything I had written during the past several months correctly. And I wondered if I'd written anything that could potentially hurt the deal from moving forward.

This day wasn't just my deposition—it was December 15, 2009, coincidentally the one-year anniversary of the day I learned Flying J was headed toward bankruptcy. I couldn't believe that it had already been a year. So much had changed. My life was completely unrecognizable from what it had been just one year ago. I had gone from managing our home life and our kids' activities to leading a major reorganization of our family business. I had been pulled from my comfort zone and I had learned so much. It would be worth all the stressful moments if I could meet my goal of paying creditors back and preserving jobs.

The deposition went very well. I was happy with the line of questioning and felt I did a decent job of listening and responding to questions. Even the journal that I had been so concerned about ended up working in our favor. It made me feel positive about the deal, until I heard a rumor that the FTC was planning to sue to fight the merger. It was just a rumor, but nonetheless disturbing. I had heard so many rumors it was becoming difficult to know what was real. I decided to wait until I heard the real decision.

As the holidays approached, I knew it was important to get a positive message out to the employees. Many of our employees had hoped the merger would not happen. Even though I knew they didn't always like the message, I felt it was my responsibility to keep them as informed as I could. I held several meetings with our Ogden employees and even put together a video with our vice president of operations that went out to the field employees. I explained our bankruptcy exit strategy, refinancing the North Salt Lake Refinery, merging with Pilot, and selling the Bakersfield Refinery. I also wanted to apologize for some of the benefits we were forced to cut, like the health reimbursement accounts. I knew that many were frustrated and nearly everyone was concerned with what these changes meant to them and their futures. I knew that I wouldn't be able to quash all of their fears or answer every question, but I had hoped to provide some relief and answers before the holidays. Even with all the uncertainty, our employees had largely stuck by me over the past year and stayed loyal to Flying J.

Meeting with my executive team on the morning of December 22, 2009, I could tell the news from the FTC wasn't positive. The rumor I'd heard was true: it was considering a lawsuit to stop the merger. It was terrible news. We immediately jumped on a call with Pilot to discuss our next plan of action. We all agreed that if the FTC decided to sue, we'd fight back in court—a move that could take years. We were hoping it didn't come to that, but we were prepared to go all the way to see this deal through. Based on the issues the FTC kept raising, it was clear that they were not taking into consideration that we were in bankruptcy and approving this merger would allow us to pay all our creditors back. Both the Pilot and Flying J teams agreed to fight and move as fast as we could to get this to court so it could be resolved.

I was concerned more than ever about keeping Flying J operations running smoothly, which meant keeping people happy and motivated—not an easy task when they were fearful for their jobs. The delay with the FTC gave employees hope that the deal would fall through, which is what many of them wanted. They wanted ownership to remain as it always had been. Many employees approached me about finding another solution, but unfortunately that wasn't a realistic option.

The only problem would be getting out of bankruptcy if the Pilot merger did not happen. As the FTC became more likely to take us to court and potentially stop our merger, we needed to engage with our current partner, ConocoPhillips, and our executives to put together a business strategy if we did *not* merge with Pilot. I put together a team of our brightest young executives, and they worked for several weeks completing a backup plan to operate the business without Pilot. The plan was complete by early June 2010.

A Comdata Resolution

While we were waiting for the FTC, there were several other hurdles that needed to be cleared before we could move forward postmerger. We were still facing legal battles with the payment processing company Comdata stemming from universally accepting their card while they accepted our TCH card.

Flying J and Comdata had a contentious relationship that extended back over a decade. Flying J had stopped accepting the Comdata card at our facilities because of high merchant rates, even though it was the most utilized card in the industry.

By not accepting Comdata cards at our travel plazas, we cut off the ability for many customers to purchase diesel or other items at our plazas. In addition, Comdata refused to accept Flying J's TCH card. Stuck at an impasse, Flying J and Comdata argued in court for several years. Flying J's position was that Comdata was violating antitrust laws by denying equal access to the market. The lawsuit was resolved in May 2001, when the court ruled in Flying J's favor and Comdata was ordered to modify its software to accept TCH cards and pay a $49 million cash settlement.

But Flying J's battles with Comdata were not officially over for several more years. In February 2006, Flying J filed another antitrust suit against Comdata, as well as TravelCenters of America (TA) and Pilot, alleging that the companies were scheming to prevent the TCH card from competing effectively with Comdata's card. In early 2009, shortly after we had announced that Flying J was filing for Chapter 11, I began a negotiation process with Comdata. I knew that we needed the antitrust lawsuit resolved so we could move forward and accept the Comdata card at our travel plazas, which could add a substantial amount of business at a time when we needed all the business we could get. My goal was to settle the case and create a mutually beneficial relationship. We would accept Comdata cards in Flying J plazas, but Comdata needed to offer a settlement.

Unfortunately, as we met it became clear that they weren't interested in settling. It was a difficult conversation—no one was seeing eye to eye or looking for a solution. The discussion turned into an "our side, your side" battle, and we were getting nowhere fast.

We decided to part ways and discuss more options with our antitrust attorneys. Our attorneys presented a case for pursuing the lawsuit. I still wondered, however, whether it made more sense to settle and accept the Comdata card in our travel plazas instead of pursuing more legal battles.

I spoke to the president of Comdata, Brett Rodewald, who said they were still interested in Flying J accepting Comdata cards and settling the lawsuit. But he made it clear that he didn't believe Comdata had any guilt in the case, which wasn't what I wanted to hear. I told him I'd fly to Nashville to meet and discuss our options. I wanted to find mutual ground that we both felt comfortable with. He agreed that it was time to settle our past differences and find a solution.

I landed in Nashville on July 1, 2009 and was greeted by Brett. I could tell right away that he was sincerely interested in working with us, though at first our discussions were quite tense. He made no effort to hide the fact that he was bothered by the lawsuit, and I couldn't blame him.

As we worked through the issues, I felt like a fish out of water. I had been so focused on the bankruptcy that I wasn't familiar with the ins and outs of the lawsuit and couldn't talk intelligently about it. But the president was patient and open. Together we would find a solution that our companies could live with.

I left Nashville with an agreement that the president would send us a proposal for Flying J to accept Comdata cards in our plazas. I told him that if it looked compelling enough we would drop the lawsuit. He seemed excited about starting a new phase in our relationship, and so was I. It was far past time to put our history with Comdata to rest and move in a productive direction. I was looking forward to developing a new, positive relationship with this long-time adversary. I believed accepting Comdata transactions in our travel plazas, which we had not done for over 10 years, would definitely boost sales.

Meanwhile, our merger with Pilot was also moving in a good direction. I told Jimmy about my hope to strike a deal with Comdata, and he was supportive. Part of our merger involved getting TCH cards into Pilot stores. Accepting Comdata cards in Flying J stores would complete the process—we would accept Comdata cards and TCH cards would be accepted everywhere. It was a positive change for the industry and customers, one in which everyone came out winners. This agreement would mean universal acceptance of all the major transportation payment options at all the major truck stop chains, giving customers many more payment options.

Unfortunately, Comdata's first proposal wasn't one we could easily accept. They proposed an approximate 1 percent fee for funded transactions and a $0.95 fee for direct bill transactions. They did not offer a settlement amount. That price was way too high and we told them so. We asked to see different pricing. We also wanted them to consider granting a signing bonus to convince us to drop the suit. It probably wouldn't amount to a lot of money, but it was something. Overall, our relationship with Comdata was moving in the right direction, and I was confident that we could reach an agreement quickly.

Over the next several months I grew to really like Brett. He was dedicated to improving Comdata, and I could tell he wanted to find a mutually beneficial arrangement with us. Though our companies had a rocky past, he didn't let it cloud his judgment or opinion of us.

In October 2009, Comdata offered us a $7.5 million settlement, an offer we could accept. We were working persistently to get Comdata cards into Flying J stores, as well as TCH cards into Pilot stores. We hoped everything would come together just as the FTC was weighing its final decision on our impending merger with Pilot.

When we learned of the FTC's delay, I decided that it might be best to negotiate the Comdata deal with Pilot. But I wasn't sure if Brett would be on board. I knew that he wasn't very pleased with the merger, and I wasn't sure how to approach the subject. But Brett beat me to the punch. He brought up the change of control and wanted to include it in the settlement as long as he could hold his 2011 pricing. Pilot was on fairly good terms with Comdata but wanted to be certain our deal with Comdata wouldn't negatively affect them. I didn't anticipate any last-minute hurdles between Comdata and Pilot, but I knew that some disagreements could arise.

ConocoPhillips was also nervous about the deal. By early 2010, it seemed as though they were the only aspect standing in our way of getting the deal with Comdata done. Comdata was negotiating directly with Pilot, and I was confident that they'd work out a deal. I wasn't as confident about ConocoPhillips. As was the case with most issues with ConocoPhillips, they were much more comfortable with the status quo than making any change, even if it seemed obvious that it would have a positive impact on Flying J.

By March 2010, Comdata and ConocoPhillips had made very little progress. I could tell that Comdata wanted to move forward. In fact, Brett requested that we agree to sign a release against ever going back in history. I knew it was risky, but I also knew it was in our best interest. Brett grew supportive of paying us the settlement, but he wasn't very enthusiastic about paying ConocoPhillips or Pilot. Still, we were making headway. It looked like our deal would be made by the end of May.

By the first of June, the Comdata card was officially up and running in 270 U.S. and Canadian Flying J travel plazas. It was an amazing feat to finally see this accomplished. I knew that our customers would have enhanced payment options and expanded access to our fuel network. I was excited to close this long chapter of Flying J's history and see how accepting the card would enhance the plazas in the future.

Transportation Clearing House– Another Piece of the Puzzle

Beyond accepting Comdata cards in our travel plazas, we needed our competitors to begin accepting our TCH card at their truck stops. When Flying J established Transportation Clearing House, our card processing company, in the mid-'90s, it was another essential step toward expanding our reach into the financial industry. The TCH card provided fuel purchase and financial management solutions for its many customers through payment cards that were accepted at thousands of truck stop and travel plaza locations throughout the United States and Canada. TCH was an innovative platform that provided cutting-edge technological solutions for fuel transactions, money transfers, and data processing. It was beneficial for Flying J and the company's many customers. But TCH wasn't well received by Flying J's competitors, including Pilot, Love's, and TravelCenters of America (TA), who refused to accept the TCH card at their facilities, opting instead to work solely with Comdata.

Universal acceptance of the TCH card was a significant problem because most trucking companies needed to purchase fuel at Pilot, Love's, or TA truck stops. Historically, TCH cards had been used by the loyal Flying J customer base, but the lack of acceptance at the other three major truck stops made it tough for fleets of significant size to use the TCH card exclusively. When TCH did win large customers they usually carried two cards (TCH and Comdata) that between them would be accepted at all truck stops. This dual-card solution seemed good in theory, but it created fraud and driver theft exposure for the fleets. The coordinated boycott of the TCH card by the three major truck stops led to the aforementioned antitrust lawsuit that extended for years. But the story had changed. We now needed—and wanted—mutual acceptance of both cards in all major plazas. In May 2008, just six months before the bankruptcy, TA agreed to accept the TCH card in conjunction with a $5 million settlement of the pending lawsuit.

As we inched closer to merging with Pilot, we knew that we needed to end the legal battles between TCH and our competitors once and for all. We wanted to find a compromise that would result in the TCH card's acceptance at Pilot and Love's locations. As part of our pending merger, we came to an agreement that Pilot would acquire 37.5 percent of TCH for $25 million.

ConocoPhillips again seemed very nervous about any deals we were striking with Pilot, and in many ways they were rightfully nervous. ConocoPhillips owned 25 percent of TCH. When Pilot agreed to acquire nearly 40 percent of TCH, ConocoPhillips was slow to come on board. They reacted similarly to when we announced Pilot would be acquiring our plazas—hesitant and cautious. But as both deals moved forward, they began to realize that Pilot's acquisition created a valuable exit strategy for their Flying J assets.

Our hope was that it would create more opportunities for TCH to expand, including universal acceptance of the card at all truck stops and travel plazas. There were still hurdles to overcome, but we ultimately came to an agreement that Pilot would acquire all of ConocoPhillips's ownership and 25 percent of our ownership in TCH, which gave them a 50 percent ownership stake instead of the original 37.5 percent, as well as accept TCH cards at its truck stops. In short, TCH was headed toward a very bright future. We still, however, needed TCH acceptance from some of our longtime competitors. Because the FTC was worried that our merger with Pilot would create market dominance, it had included a premerger stipulation requiring that some Pilot and Flying J travel plazas be sold to our competitors. Since we were already in talks with Love's regarding acquiring several of the plazas, I decided to approach Love's CEO Frank Love about his company's acceptance of TCH cards. With Flying J preparing to accept Comdata cards, TA now accepting the cards, and Pilot on board to accept them as well, it made sense that Love's would see an opportunity to accept TCH cards in their stores. By accepting the cards, Love's would be opening their doors to TCH's numerous customers.

Love's was open to our strategy and proposal. They saw how it made sense to work with us. Love's was honest about their concerns about how accepting the card would impact their business. Moreover, they were worried about changes to the card once the Pilot and Flying J deal was done.

By the end of April 2010, we had reached a deal with Love's, and they officially began accepting TCH cards on June 26, 2010. Shortly afterward, on July 2, 2010, Pilot officially began accepting the TCH card. TCH finally had universal acceptance, eliminating the biggest obstacle in its path to significant growth.

These breakthroughs were crucial turning points for TCH. With Love's, TA, and Pilot on board, it was only a matter of time before all travel plazas and truck stops would accept the card. Universal acceptance would open numerous opportunities for TCH in the future.

Alon USA Energy Acquires the Bakersfield Refinery

During the summer of 2009, the Bakersfield Refinery was put through an auction process and Alon USA Energy had won with the highest bid. As I spoke to the Alon CEO in late summer of 2009, I learned that the company's acquisition intent was real, but they had no financial backing for their offer. They were determined to acquire the property and assured us they would get the necessary funding. While the CEO sounded eager to get the deal done, I knew I couldn't believe it just yet. Fred Greener, our president of refining, spent the next several months going back and forth with Alon trying to strike a deal that would work.

Unfortunately, we experienced setback after setback, and we were nowhere close to finalizing Alon's Bakersfield Refinery acquisition by the end of 2009. It was still in our best interest for Alon to move on Bakersfield, since it was key to our reorganization plan, so we tried to remain patient with their process. My goal was to do whatever it took to close the deal by December 31, 2009. But the ball was in Alon's court.

We started the new year without a deal signed. It seemed like Alon was stalling. Even though the refinery was not processing any crude oil, we were still paying the $3 million cost to keep the refinery warm each month. Since we had no other companies pursuing the purchase of Bakersfield, if the deal with Alon fell through we would have wasted millions of dollars. I grew impatient and decided to put a deadline in place to shut down the refinery. I said that if a deal were not signed, I would announce to the press we were shutting down the refinery the last week of January 2010. I'm not sure if I would really have had the guts to shut it down and quash any hope of ever selling it, but we couldn't afford to keep it warm at $3 million a month. Moreover, I needed Alon to believe I was serious.

My plan worked, and we received word from Alon that they were prepared to sign the very next day. If all went as planned, we'd have a deal. And it actually happened. On January 27, 2010, Alon signed the paperwork and the acquisition was officially in motion. Moreover, the courts agreed to the Bakersfield Refinery sale.

On June 1, 2010, Alon officially acquired the Bakersfield Refinery. The purchase price was $40 million in cash. Though lower than we originally anticipated, it was our only option at the time. Included in the acquisition was the Bakersfield Refinery's existing inventory as of the closing date of the transaction.

Acquiring the Bakersfield Refinery for $40 million was a great deal for Alon. It was painful to take such a financial loss—we had purchased Bakersfield for $120 million and invested several hundred million more in engineering and equipment. Over the next few years we were able to extract another $15 million by selling all the emission credits owned by the Bakersfield Refinery. In 2018 we sold the last of the land near the refinery for $9 million. Our full recovery for our Bakersfield endeavor was less than $100 million, leaving our losses at over $600 million. These losses, resulting from the decision to start an expensive project before the proper permits were in place, were likely one of the main reasons for the bankruptcy.

I received another vote of confidence that our plan to exit bankruptcy was working when Bank of America approached us in August, just nine months after defaulting on their loans had put us into bankruptcy, to potentially help us refinance our North Salt Lake Refinery debt. If we could get this financing done, we could keep one of our best assets. Because of the struggles with the FTC, the credit committee wanted us to put the North Salt Lake Refinery up for sale even though we would not need to if the Pilot merger happened. I quietly put the North Salt Lake Refinery on the auction block, and hoped all would work out so that we could refinance the debt and keep it.

We celebrated the 2010 New Year knowing that Flying J had a solid plan to exit out of bankruptcy. In addition to having our deal signed with Pilot, we had Bakersfield lined up, we had completed the sales of Longhorn and Flying J Oil and Gas, and we had early indications that Bank of America would agree to the refinancing of the North Salt Lake Refinery. ConocoPhillips had also completed selling their ownership stake in CFJ to Pilot. Everything we had worked so hard to accomplish during the past several months was finally coming together.

Love's and TravelCenters of America

When the FTC finally came forward with a plan other than suing us, it included divesting properties to another large player. The FTC's willingness to consider divestiture as an option gave us hope the deal could be done. The requirement would alleviate concerns the FTC had about antitrust implications. In early February 2010,

Jimmy sent the FTC a list of 24 stores for divestiture. The FTC wanted the stores to all go to one company, and it had to be either Love's or TravelCenters of America. Jimmy's list included several Flying J stores, but the one that made me the saddest was our Salt Lake plaza, since it was a hometown store. When I brought this to Jimmy's attention, he quickly switched our Salt Lake Flying J store for his Pilot store—yet another gesture that assured me he cared about our future relationship.

We approached Love's and TA about acquiring plazas throughout the country. Both were interested in the opportunity, but on terms that weren't totally acceptable. We knew, however, that both Love's and TA had too many upsides to derail the deal by not buying the stores we'd need to sell them.

Love's expressed more interest than TA, but they were also driving a hard bargain. In April 2010, Love's informed us that they wanted five more sites—a deal that neither Jimmy nor I could get behind.

I flew to Oklahoma City to meet with Frank Love and discuss the potential deal. It was clear that he wasn't willing to pay much more than his original offer, which was remarkably low, even with the additional stores he wanted included in the deal. It was not in our interest to include more stores, but it was what the FTC wanted. Moreover, we didn't have much of a choice. We needed the Love's contract done.

By May we had made a lot of headway with Love's, and I was confident that we'd reach an agreement. Love's was positive about accepting TCH but didn't want to negotiate on price when it came to acquiring the plazas. They had put forth a figure that was lower than what Jimmy and I felt comfortable with, but they seemingly weren't willing to budge. While I was confident that Love's TCH deal would go through, I was beginning to lose hope that they would acquire some plazas. I had lost hope that TA would acquire plazas long ago, which meant Love's was the only bidder—an advantage that they were well aware of. There was no way they were going to pay what we believed to be market price for the plazas. It was an especially tough negotiation for Jimmy, who had little ability to work a better deal with Love's since they knew how badly he wanted our merger to happen. It went back and forth for several weeks, but by early June, Love's officially acquired six Flying J properties and 19 Pilot properties.

Our Day in Court

Principle: You always win
when you act with integrity.

The Merger Is Final

On June 30, 2010, I went to the office knowing that this was the day we were to hear from the FTC. At this point we were confident that they were planning to approve the deal. My executive team gathered in my office waiting for the phone to ring, which we were expecting to happen at 10 a.m. Finally around noon we got the call: the FTC had approved our merger with Pilot. Everyone moved full speed ahead to get the required paperwork filed by the end of the day. We had finally reached our goal of merging our two companies, which would allow Flying J to pay our creditors back in full. Pilot was ready to go on day one. They had been working on a transition plan for a year, so when the deal was officially done they were able to move rapidly to incorporate Flying J's assets into their operations.

185

For our employees, who had patiently waited to see how our reorganization would work out, this was not a happy day. So on one hand I was thrilled and relieved that we would pay our creditors back and many field employees would keep their jobs, but on the other hand I was extremely sad for those employees in our Ogden headquarters whose futures were now more uncertain than ever. Many were given the required 60-day notice of termination on the first day of the merger. The outcome for the employees was by far the most sad and disappointing outcome of my tenure as CEO at Flying J and to date in my career.

On July 6, 2010, my Flying J team traveled to Delaware to present our plan of reorganization to the court. Our plan included 100 percent payment with interest to all creditors. The Pilot merger was the cornerstone of our plan, putting several million dollars into our coffers along with the proceeds from the sale of the Bakersfield Refinery, the Longhorn Pipeline, and other smaller subsidiaries that did not make long-term sense to hang on to.

After presenting our reorganization plan to Judge Mary F. Walrath of the U.S. Bankruptcy Court, she responded with the following:

> I think you are too modest in suggesting [its] significance . . . given where you started 18 months ago and where you are ending up now. I don't think anybody would have anticipated the amount of recovery for creditors. And I know it's due to lots of effort behind the scenes, and I appreciate it. By all accounts, the resolution of Flying J's bankruptcy was atypical. Most insolvent companies are liquidated or dismantled piece by piece to settle their debts. Businesses that survive usually can't repay their debts in full, a black mark that can haunt them for years.

The Chapter 11 team in front of the U.S. Bankruptcy Court in Wilmington, Delaware, July 2010 (left to right): Scott Clayson, John Kaufman, Flip Hufford, David Eaton, John Boken, Andre Lortz, Chuck and Crystal Maggelet, Chris Malan, Brett Bailey, Adam Paul, Edmond Morton, and unidentified.

Her statement meant so much to me and the entire team. We had started from such dismal circumstances, not knowing exactly how we would find our way out of the bankruptcy mess—but we found our way. We remained committed to solving each problem, even if it meant tackling just one issue at a time, one day at a time. We never lost the motivation to work hard until we could come out of the bankruptcy, and we never lost the foresight to make decisions that kept our integrity intact.

On July 23, 2010, the reorganization plan was approved. That was the day we had all been waiting for since learning of Flying J's mounting troubles that culminated in its Chapter 11 bankruptcy in December 2008. We were all relieved and happy that this chapter in Flying J's history had finally come to a close.

It was a gratifying moment in our company history and for me on a personal level. The plan of reorganization and the merger with Pilot created a stronger version of what the company had been. In July 2010, Flying J received $500 million in cash and a 12.7 percent stake in the merged company valued at $1.19 billion. Within six months after closing we repurchased equity to raise our ownership stake to about 18 percent. Unlike many companies who go through bankruptcy, we exited with many operating businesses intact, with much less debt, and with cash. In addition, we still fully owned and controlled the North Salt Lake Refinery, TAB, and 50 percent of TCH. Pilot Flying J was now accepting the Comdata card, and our former competitors were now accepting TCH—it was a winning solution for all companies and customers.

Though it wasn't always easy to accept the merger, I still believe merging with Pilot was the best decision that we could have made given the circumstances Flying J was in. I had been committed to paying all creditors back from the beginning of the bankruptcy, but there wasn't always a clear path to how we would accomplish such a gigantic goal. Yet here we were, less than two years after our bankruptcy filing and able to pay our nearly 6,000 creditors back in full.

As we celebrated our exit from bankruptcy, I was surprised that there were some who questioned our decisions to ensure each and every creditor was paid back. I have heard statements such as, "Why didn't you take advantage of the bankruptcy? You didn't have to pay everyone back." To our family and executives, hiding behind the bankruptcy so we wouldn't have to pay our creditors was never an option. I was and remain proud of our decision and ability to exit bankruptcy with our credibility, integrity, and values intact. To me, that aspect was more important than nearly any other part of our journey.

It was a proud moment when I was awarded the Ernest Shackleton Award by our investment bankers at our closing dinner to celebrate

The Ernest Shackleton Award, presented to Crystal at the bankruptcy closing dinner by The Blackstone Group, October 2010.

our success. Shackleton was an early-twentieth-century explorer who attempted to cross Antarctica from sea to sea via the pole in 1914–17. Disaster struck when the expedition's ship, *Endurance*, became trapped in pack ice and was slowly crushed before the shore parties could land. The crew escaped by camping on the sea ice until it disintegrated, then launching lifeboats to reach Elephant Island in the Southern Ocean and ultimately the inhabited island of South Georgia in the South Atlantic Ocean, a stormy ocean voyage of 720 nautical miles and Shackleton's most famous exploit. No one believed they would survive, but under Shackleton's leadership they prevailed.

The reason given for awarding me this trophy came from Blackstone's belief that, like Shackleton, I was able to take on a seemingly impossible task and guide our team to a very positive outcome.

Settling Claims

The company's next step of action was to resolve our creditors' claims. We still had about 120 claims to negotiate and several thousand to process, totaling close to $2 billion.

Throughout the course of the bankruptcy I knew that I wanted to be the kind of business executive who treated people and businesses with the respect they deserved, thus informing my decision to pay all creditors back what was rightfully owed to them. Though I believed in this philosophy, I learned this lesson again when meeting with Berry Petroleum, a company that had been greatly impacted by our bankruptcy. I knew that we owed them around $40 million, and I wanted to give them a fair claim. They, however, wanted more than I had anticipated, including compensation for lost production and a terminated contract. I inched up our settlement offer to $50 million, thinking it was a fair deal. They, on the other hand, wanted $67 million, an amount I was nowhere near close to agreeing upon. But over the next hour I listened to how our company's failures had cost them dearly. Our situation almost led to their own bankruptcy and demise. They too had faced hard times in late 2008 and they had been relying on our crude payment to pay their bills. Without it they had to scramble. They were a small company doing business with us in good faith, and we had let them down. Though I had never planned to exceed a $50 million offer, I ended up giving them $60 million.

As we paid off each creditor during the next several months, it felt good restoring the trust and reputation that Flying J had nearly lost during the tumultuous times of the bankruptcy. By the end of 2010 we had paid back every creditor.

In order to keep the Flying J brand with the travel plazas, Pilot agreed to call the new company Pilot Flying J. Giving up our plazas was not easy for me. My dad and his team had built those plazas—many from the ground up. They had developed an expansive network of stops throughout the United States and Canada.

But beyond dotting the map, our plazas had a reputation of being the best in the industry. Truckers grew to expect clean, efficient, technologically innovative plazas. We understood customer service and we prided ourselves on being the home away from home for small professional drivers. We even referred to the travel plaza part of our business as "highway hospitality." We catered to the owner/operator. Pilot had a different philosophy. They courted large trucking companies, which then instructed their drivers where to stop. I suspected this difference would be the biggest and most painful obstacle the companies would face when they came together as one.

Since the time my dad opened the first Flying J fueling stop in 1968, his company grew to become one of Utah's largest family-owned companies. Moreover, it grew to become a household name, with a brand that was recognized throughout the industry and by patrons across the country. But more than just an enormously successful operation, Flying J had become an integral part of the lives of its thousands of employees. One of the most difficult aspects of our merger with Pilot was not just saying good-bye to the Flying J company as it had been, but recognizing that the merger would have a profound impact on the lives of our employees, many of whom had been loyal Flying J employees for decades. Most of our field employees continued to be employed by Pilot Flying J, but many at the Ogden headquarters were no longer needed and lost their jobs.

By the end of August 2010 we had either laid off or transferred nearly our entire Ogden staff. Many of our employees—many of whom were now *former* employees—didn't understand why the bankruptcy had led to this outcome. They thought I was selling out—that it wasn't necessary to merge with Pilot. Flying J had become part of their identity. They were proud when they said they worked for Flying J. The company's name meant something to them and to the community. Although the brand would live on along America's interstates, for them it would never be the same. It was different for me, because I would serve on the Pilot Flying J board and have a minority ownership stake. I also could keep the legacy alive by building from the past culture of the remaining part of the company we still controlled.

On the day that I knew was the last day for many of our Ogden staff, I attended the checkout process so that I could meet with them one on one, shake their hands, and thank them for their service. I was expecting the event to be filled with gloom but was pleasantly surprised with how positive and upbeat most people were. Repeatedly I heard comments from employees who had considered the Flying J change to be an opportunity for them to pursue something in their own lives. I heard, for example, from a woman who decided to turn this time into an opportunity to pursue her lifelong dream of becoming a nurse. Another individual told me how excited he was to be able to spend more time with his family. I was inspired to see so many people turning a potentially negative situation into something positive.

On November 5, 2012, nearly four years after Flying J entered Chapter 11 bankruptcy, my dad was inducted into the Utah Business Hall of Fame. I got a bit emotional as I accepted the award on his behalf. It was a privilege to speak to the audience to honor his many accomplishments. What I said still resonates with me today:

> *This award is an honor to my father, but I know if he were standing here tonight he would say that those that deserve the credit are the individuals that so closely worked with him. My dad had a unique skill that many*

entrepreneurs do not possess. He had no problem allowing others to do their jobs with little management from him. I believe this is why Flying J grew as large and as quickly as it did. Today, most small start-up companies are sold by the founder, and the person is left behind as others used to managing larger businesses take the person's idea and grow large companies. In Jay's case, he invested in people and believed as a team the executives could build a great company. I have heard many Flying J executives tell stories of how they asked my father how he wanted something done and he simply said do what you think.

When mistakes were made, he would tell people to just get over the mistake, learn from it and move on. When he sent me a business plan while I was living back East and said he wondered if I would be interested in coming back to Utah to build a hotel, I knew this would be my opportunity and that Dad would not stand in my way. For years while Chuck, my husband, and I built our hotel business, my dad stood by as a silent investor, only stepping in when we asked him for specific advice.

My father was a very intelligent man and a gentle soul. He loved to fly around in his airplane all over the U.S. looking for new sites to build truck stops. Along the way he would meet all kinds of people. He loved to visit with them.

When I travel to Flying Js today, I am often told stories by our employees about the day Jay Call landed his helicopter in the parking lot and then took them for a ride. It is usually a clerk or maintenance person telling me this story and it is the highlight of their life. Jay loved everyone and he always made them feel at ease talking to him.

He never considered himself to be any better than anyone else. Anyone that knew Jay at all knew he was a clean freak. If he traveled to one of the plazas and the floor was dirty, instead of asking for someone to clean it he would ask for the supplies and clean it himself. He became successful through hard work and a keen eye for opportunity.

When I was in high school I told my dad I did not believe that there was any more opportunity left for my generation. He laughed and said there is opportunity everywhere: "Crystal, you only have to keep your eyes open." Today I know he was right, and I truly believe, as he did, that hard work, preparing yourself for any opportunity, and the willingness to take chances when an opportunity presents itself leads to success.

In my mind Jay was an amazing businessman. He worked hard to strike deals that were fair to everyone involved. He believed that the only successful deal was a deal that both people felt good about when it was complete. I try every day to live up to the standards in the business world that my father set. There are very few weeks that go by in my current role at FJ Management that someone doesn't come up to me and say they knew my dad and admired the man he was. Most of them tell me a story about how they interacted together. I am amazed at the lives he touched in his 62 years. I know my dad would be very appreciative of the recognition tonight.

My dad was an inspirational business leader with a powerful vision. He helped shape an industry and influenced many lives. As I look back, I am in awe of what he accomplished.

Now that several years have passed since Flying J and Pilot merged, I look back with pride that I dared to trust Jimmy against all my advisors' recommendations. We were in a lawsuit, and I didn't like the rumors floating of a pending sale before we had even begun discussions. But Jimmy kept trying; the more he talked and the more I listened, the more I began to believe I could trust him. It's hard to say if it's a good thing to trust people before you really know them, and I hope I'll always be one who was trusted by others. I strive to give everyone the benefit of the doubt. People don't have to earn my trust—they have my trust from the beginning until they do something to lose it.

I carried this personal philosophy with me in all of my dealings throughout the bankruptcy, including my work with Jimmy. He was high energy and easy to talk to. When we finally reached our tentative deal in July 2009, I was excited by the prospect of having a partner I could trust, someone with years of experience in our industry to take our company to places neither of us had ever dreamed of.

Even with such a competitive past, Jimmy was a man of his word. Of course he always had *his* company at the top of his priority list, but I could tell that he sincerely cared about Flying J. Throughout our journey I never doubted that he was working toward our favor as well as Pilot's. And he found a way to make both sides reach a successful and mutually beneficial position. Not only did Jimmy have to negotiate with me and all the concerned parties that surrounded me, he also had to structure a deal with ConocoPhillips and work with the FTC. I credit the merger's success to Jimmy's honest, open work ethic, and his determination and patience to see a deal he had dreamed of through to the end.

The newly created company, Pilot Flying J, included an expanded network of more than 550 interstate travel plazas with operations in 43 states and 6 Canadian provinces and more than 20,000 employees. It immediately became one of the top 10 largest privately held companies in the United States.

Not only did I have to trust many people, many people had to trust me. In addition to all the creditors, employees, and advisors who eventually put their trust in me, two others, my stepmother, Tamra, and my brother, Thad, also stood by my side knowing my leadership was directly impacting their futures.

Tamra Call

Aside from the lifelong influence of my mother, my stepmother, Tamra, had been a rock for me and strengthened my confidence throughout the bankruptcy, especially when times were tough. The death of my father was extremely difficult for Tamra. Not only had she lost her husband, but the stability of her finances was now in jeopardy. Widowed at 50 years old, Tamra was left with a large ranch in an isolated area in Montana. My father and her traveled in and out of the ranch by airplane, which now, not knowing how to fly herself, left Tamra quite isolated. Though Tamra owned the ranch, it had been leased by Flying J and she had received their payment monthly to pay for property expenses. But now Flying J no longer had a need for the property, so Tamra was responsible for all the expenses and upkeep on the ranch that had been handled by hired hands in the past. She had a difficult time transitioning into this new lifestyle that she had not signed on for. Though my stepmom had lived at the ranch for several years, she was accustomed to a support team to care for the ranch and all the expenses.

Watching her face the huge challenges of losing her husband and then years later having her inheritance compromised was heartbreaking to me. However, I was also empowered by her courage to handle these tragedies by learning how to support herself. Each time there was a setback she learned what she needed to do to move on and get her life back on track.

Often she was in the middle of her own crisis and way out of her comfort zone when she would reach out to support me during the bankruptcy and the company's restructuring. She never questioned my decisions or choices for the future of the company, or my handling of the bankruptcy of her late husband's company. She never took the bankruptcy, how I handled it, or the saving of the company for granted. I appreciated her support, even though she had plenty of stress to manage in her own life.

Thad Call

Although my brother, Thad, always showed support and trust, the story that did not spread to the public was the private crisis my family was handling at the same time as our financial crisis. During the height of the bankruptcy, an intoxicated Thad fell and hit his head. He was placed in an induced coma after extensive brain surgery. Thad was able to recover, but his attitude toward his addiction did not change. He chose to live life hard and fast. He no longer was interested in working with the company. Though he remained on the board of directors and was a major stockholder, he left the decision-making completely up to me. His fun lifestyle left no time to come into the office to build the company.

A year later, in 2011, Thad hit his head again and was back in the hospital. He didn't need surgery this time, but he had to take Coumadin to treat an intracranial hematoma. He was cautioned at that time that he needed to stay away from alcohol. But his bad habits and addictions were too ingrained, and now with what he perceived as unlimited monetary means, he had no compelling reason to change his lifestyle.

I began getting very frustrated with my brother. Unlike many alcoholics, he would never hit rock bottom. He placed alcohol as a first priority in his life. He had two very smart, successful children and many reasons to live, but he chose to jeopardize his health by drinking. He had all the money he needed to live an ostentatious lifestyle, building large homes and traveling the world. I would often say he was the smart one because I worked to keep and grow our family business and he enjoyed the financial rewards it provided.

I came to accept the fact that he was going to live his life on his own terms. No amount of discussion or pleading from me, our mom, his wife, kids, friends, or extended family was going to get him to change his ways. It had to come from him, and he wasn't interested. So I continued to keep him and his family involved in our family business and apprised of board meetings, but his attendance at board and family functions became less and less. He was never critical of decisions we made with the business and was generally appreciative of his ability to have access to wealth.

On June 9, 2018, he fell and hit his head and died. It was the call I had anticipated for several years, but had always hoped I wouldn't receive. Mostly I felt sorry for his children, who had to watch their father's mental and physical abilities diminish over several years. He leaves behind a great legacy in his children and grandchildren.

Identity Crisis

Principle: Don't look in the rearview mirror; work toward a new start.

O ne of the most significant changes I faced in the earliest days following the merger and bankruptcy exit was balancing my leadership role at FJ Management with my new and somewhat undefined responsibilities at Pilot Flying J, where I was serving in an advisory position. My goal in staying engaged in the merger was to help unite the two former competing companies into one congruent organization. I hoped to help determine best practices from each company and keep the best from both organizations.

During the first several weeks I traveled with Jimmy Haslam around the country to visit with past Flying J employees who were now Pilot Flying J employees. My hope was that Pilot would adopt some of the innovative programs and processes that Flying J had perfected over the years. I worked diligently to explain the benefits of Flying J's most valuable programs, such as the Frequent Fueler Loyalty Program, which had been essential to our longtime customers. I also tried to convince Pilot to integrate some of our most innovative technological tools and strategies, like providing customers with free Wi-Fi access and scanning services.

When Pilot informed me that they weren't going to continue to use ROSS (our legacy point-of-sale system), I was surprised and somewhat dismayed. Part of the reason Flying J's brand was so strong was due to the many innovations that we had developed and perfected along the way. Despite the mistakes Phil Adams had made over the years, one thing was clear: he was a visionary who brought a lot of unique ideas to the company and to the entire industry. Though we had experienced a severe hardship during the past year, Flying J was successful for decades because we had a legacy of innovation, and it was difficult seeing our offerings disregarded, especially when I knew that they would greatly benefit the joint venture.

Jimmy encouraged me to participate in the newly formed company, and I stayed very much a part of PFJ for the first year. I traveled to Pilot's Knoxville headquarters frequently, participated in several meetings, conventions, and teleconferences, and gave my two cents whenever appropriate. I strived to remain actively involved in PFJ to help keep the Flying J brand alive and relevant. But I soon came to recognize that PFJ was under Pilot's command, and there wasn't much I could do.

Beyond our products and processes, our people on the ground also struggled to merge into the new operation. Many of Flying J's longtime managers were moved to smaller Pilot stores, while the Pilot managers moved to larger Flying J stores. I am certain it was frustrating to our managers, and few remained at PFJ after only a few years. With this said, even though I do not agree with everything that went on at PFJ, the merged company quickly became extremely successful in spite of leaving Flying J programs behind.

Participating with PFJ was a small part of my responsibilities once we exited bankruptcy in July 2010. One of the first steps we needed to take was determining our new name. We wanted to choose a name that paid homage to the company's legacy while also being careful not to sound too close to the Flying J name itself. It was important to me that the Flying J name and brand live on at the travel plazas. I wanted Pilot to use the Flying J name as much as possible. To avoid confusion I believed it would be best to rebrand our reorganized company as something completely different. While still in U.S. Bankruptcy Court, we settled on FJ Management (FJM) and our legacy logo.

The reorganized FJ Management was a new company with employees and operations to manage. Suddenly it was not clear exactly what our future would be like, but we were positioned to rebuild and move on. The Flying J that I had known for my entire life—the fully integrated oil company that my dad had built over four decades—was gone, but the company was far from dead. As we emerged from bankruptcy, there was enormous opportunity to reinvent our company as one that would embrace the legacy of Flying J while also becoming a new organization with a different mission and new goals. Now it was up to me and the executive team to determine what the company was going to become.

Only a few days after the bankruptcy was over, I decided it was very important to me to formally have Chuck join the FJ Management executive team. He had been working by my side for the past 18 months with no title and no salary, pitching in to help any way he could with FJ and at home. I knew he would be an essential addition to the executive team to help reorganize our FJ assets.

With board and family support, Chuck moved into an executive position in addition to his board membership. Upon our exit from bankruptcy Chuck became the new chief operating officer of FJ Management. It was great to finally have him officially back working by my side. He would also take a place on the North Salt Lake Refinery board and become chairman of the board at TAB.

Overnight we were whittled down from a huge company with over 10 thousand employees and lots of advisors helping us navigate our future to approximately a thousand people who worked for TAB, TCH, and Big West. Our corporate office had been reduced from nearly 200 employees to a mere 30. When I had become CEO, we already had all kinds of very smart bankruptcy advisors there to help navigate our situation. Now that the threat of liquidation was gone and our creditors were paid back we no longer needed the highly compensated advisors, yet our future was left undetermined, posing enormous challenges and also enormous potential.

As we looked at our subsidiaries, the question now was how did they all fit together? And more importantly, what did the future of FJ Management look like? How could we unite all these very different companies, or should we even try?

We at FJ Management began examining what our core competencies had morphed into. We were no longer one of the country's largest diesel fuel providers, nor did we have much to do with hauling freight. We had transformed into a holding company that needed to support its subsidiaries as they strived to accomplish their missions and goals as independent, stand-alone businesses. To this end we decided it would be best to adopt a more decentralized organization. The biggest change this would bring to the subsidiaries would be implementing their own accounting and IT systems. The only functions we would keep centralized were human resources, payroll, and benefits.

Expanding Our Vision

As I stepped into FJ Management's Ogden-based headquarters every morning during the first years that followed the bankruptcy, I walked past Flying J's guiding principles that were etched on the doors—Opportunity, Independence, Vision, Integrity. Memories of Flying J were everywhere, reminding me and all our employees of what the company once was. In some ways it was inspiring to be surrounded by the historic images and ideals that my father had created decades ago. He was truly an inspirational leader, and while I didn't want to lose his memory or the philosophies that Flying J was founded upon, as the leader of FJ Management, I needed to define our future. We were no longer Flying J. We needed to create our own mission statement and vision.

Toward the end of 2012, I brought together a selection of executives and employees from all our subsidiaries to develop our new vision and guiding principles. We worked to come up with a list of possibilities that would work for every division of FJ Management. We wanted a statement that would celebrate our past while demonstrating our commitment to responsible growth in the future. The company's recent stormy past was still fresh on our minds and we wanted our focus to be steeped in a tradition of managing our assets in a way that built long-term value for our shareholders, our employees, and our customers. Flying J defined itself and focused on the top line—revenue growth. FJ Management decided to focus on the *bottom* line—profit. We don't want to grow merely for the sake of growth. We don't care about being on *Forbes*'s top ten list. We care about profitability and responsibly growing a company that makes a difference and survives into the future.

Our new approach was to always consider the lasting impact that one seemingly simple decision can have, and we created the mission statement Building Value to Last, with the guiding principles of Integrity, Mutual Respect, and Excellence, to be used across our companies.

When we announced our new mission statement to our employees, the theme seemed to resonate with them. Most of the employees had been with FJ Management for many years. They had been there as Flying J soared to great heights and watched as the company came falling down during 2008 and 2009. Our hope was that this new mission statement would reflect FJ Management's dedication to creating a stable future grounded by strategic and responsible growth. It was exciting to see how passionate and committed many employees were to understanding the new mission and helping to direct the company forward.

Renewing Our Focus on Employees

For years, Flying J had a go-go-go mentality, which meant it was fun to work there because there were numerous growth opportunities. How we would continue to provide these opportunities was not clear to me, but I knew that we couldn't turn FJ Management into a strong organization without empowering our employees.

We spent a lot of time discussing what was best for the employees. This was at a time when many companies were cutting their benefits due to the effects of the Great Recession coupled with increased health-care costs associated with the Affordable Care Act. Now that FJ Management was on solid ground, we weren't interested in cutting our employees' benefits. We knew that creating a positive work environment with robust benefits was a win-win for FJ Management and our employees. I wanted the company and our subsidiaries to be a place where employees could stay throughout the duration of their careers. I wanted to be the employer who people were proud to work for. We knew—and still know—that our employees are at the core of who we are as a company, and we remain dedicated to taking care of them and their families. We decided to implement a robust 401(k) program with a higher match rate, create a profit-sharing plan, and work toward rebuilding our health plans. In just a few short years, we would even implement health-care clinics at our worksites—another innovative benefit we were proud to offer our employees.

Communication was key as we tried to repair morale and establish a new culture. I had worked hard during the bankruptcy to keep all 11,000 employees informed of what was going on. When the crisis was over, I didn't communicate as well as I had during the bankruptcy, naïvely believing everyone would know it was okay. Part of the problem is that I had made the earlier decision to cut back our Human Resources Department. This meant we only had one HR executive for all our employees, down to around 1,000 at this point, and no on-site representative at any of our subsidiaries. Under this model, communication suffered, which was another blow to morale. Though I tried to communicate through the presidents of each subsidiary, I later learned that information rarely made it past one or two layers—the people on the ground were often left in the dark regarding company updates, which led to more uncertainty and trepidation. At the time I didn't understand where their fear stemmed from. We were paying well, including bonuses. We had enhanced benefits. FJ Management as a whole was headed in a very positive direction. I didn't recognize that I hadn't effectively communicated our success and stability throughout the company.

It was through this learning curve that I grew to appreciate the value of HR and realized that each entity deserved its own HR person or department. It was becoming obvious that one representative couldn't be all things to all people and all divisions. So as we began focusing on how we could better support our subsidiaries, we also assigned dedicated people to represent HR in each company. This was a welcome addition I saw as I frequently met with leadership from the North Salt Lake Refinery, TCH, and TAB. The additional HR representatives began to make a difference with communication.

I wanted to meet and get to know every employee that worked at FJ Management or one of our subsidiaries. I knew that this wouldn't be easy, but I devised a plan to make it happen. I created a monthly anniversary lunch, where all employees celebrating a milestone anniversary with the company were invited to attend lunch with me. It was a little slow at the beginning—I think employees were a bit apprehensive about lunching with the major stockholder and boss. But in the past several years it has really taken off. It's been a great experience getting to know the many people who work for our companies. It's been an eye-opening experience to hear what they like and dislike about the company, as well as to know a little about who they are outside of work. It's a great way to stay connected and maintain a focus on what really matters—our people.

Our strategy of having decentralized companies began to take hold, and our subsidiaries each became successful with their own strategies and goals.

North Salt Lake Refinery

The North Salt Lake Refinery was our cash cow before and after the bankruptcy. The refinery had a total capacity of 30,000 barrels per day and refined a combination of Utah and Wyoming crude oils to produce gasoline and diesel petroleum products for the Mountain

West market. We were able to keep the refinery by refinancing $375 million of debt. We were extremely fortunate to hold onto the refinery throughout the Flying J reorganization. It has some of our most loyal and long-term employees. I was grateful that we were able to keep it under our ownership, especially when so many people advised that I sell it.

I clearly remember being very focused on keeping all the retail facilities. I couldn't imagine selling my dad's travel plazas. During a board meeting one day, Thad said, "Crystal I don't know why you feel so determined to keep the retail facilities." I had a pecking order of companies to sell and the retail facilities were last on my list. Thad said we should keep the North Salt Lake Refinery, and he was dead on! I just thought we had to keep the family name and the family brand. To me that was my dad's legacy. Thad was seeing the bigger picture of saving the most valuable asset.

We prioritized paying the refinery debt off as soon as possible. In December 2010 we refinanced the debt, cutting the interest rate from 9.5 percent to 5.5 percent. We cut the rate by half again in April 2011. By June 2012 the debt was completely paid off. I was amazed that we were able to pay it off so quickly.

Another important step we took at the refinery was to reevaluate its safety and reliability. We had not put much capital into maintaining the refinery for several years; it was time to invest in Big West. The North Salt Lake Refinery executive team put together a robust plan that would require several hundreds of millions of dollars in capital over a 5- to 10-year time frame.

One of my proudest memories is when our North Salt Lake Refinery maintenance supervisor presented me and Chuck with an award at our annual company party. The plaque on the award read, "Our heartfelt gratitude for your leadership and your vision."

TCH/EFS

For TCH, the merger created amazing opportunity, because it was now accepted by nearly all major truck stops and fueling companies throughout the United States and Canada. It was wonderful to finally see industry-wide acceptance of TCH. It benefited not just FJ Management, but also our many TCH customers. With critical mass established, TCH was brimming with opportunity.

One of the first changes implemented at TCH was changing its fee structure. For decades the trucking credit card processing industry had used percentage-based fees. Our competitors, such as EFS Transportation Services and Comdata, were charging a 2 percent base fee at all truck stops. TCH, on the other hand, was charging a $1 flat fee per transaction. For years, TCH management pushed to match the industry standard of a 2 percent base fee, but Flying J executives never wanted to instigate the fee structure change, so the card fee remained a flat $1 per transaction. This made the card attractive for truck stop acceptance, since it was cheap compared to other cards. But with the universal acceptance of the TCH card, the flat fee no longer made any sense. TCH needed to change its truck stop fees to make it more competitive within the industry. With higher truck stop fees, TCH could offer lower and more competitive fees to trucking companies to help drive volume. In 2010, just a few short months after we exited from bankruptcy, TCH moved to the 2 percent base fee to better align with the rest of the industry.

Though our relationship with Pilot was stronger than ever, there were some frustrating aspects to it, particularly in regard to TCH, of which Pilot now owned a 50 percent share. Though we were fifty-fifty partners, it frequently felt as if Pilot had assumed full ownership of TCH, especially when it made decisions without our input. In the beginning, Pilot management changed TCH's

Sales Department. They brought in their own team and began to change the focus away from card processing and toward another technology that required capital, diverting the attention of the current management.

At Pilot's request we brought in a new CEO at TCH, Scott Phillips. Luckily Scott understood that card processing was much more important than the new technology, and he pushed to get back to the basics. He was also instrumental in TCH's 2011 merger with EFS Transportation Services, which was a huge advancement for TCH. EFS Transportation Services had a long history in the transportation card processing business and did not have an affiliation with any truck stop operators; TCH brought new innovation to the merged company. Together, these two complementary organizations formed a second-level competitor behind Comdata. The name TCH had been so closely tied to Flying J that it was decided it would be best to drop that name altogether. The new company was called Electronic Funds Source, which abbreviated as EFS, shared the same initials as its other parent company. Pilot and FJM would each now own only a third of the new company, with First Data Resources owning the other third. We now had a small stake in a larger organization. With all the changes and the new CEO being in Nashville, I was worried EFS would move out of Ogden. But I believed it would create more opportunities for the business and its employees—possibly just not in Ogden. With a stable partnership and strong leadership in place, I was hopeful that EFS would succeed. On November 15, 2011, the deal was signed and the merger was finalized. The most difficult part of the merger was giving up the TCH name in favor of EFS. Though I understood that EFS had greater market recognition, it was difficult saying good-bye to another Flying J brand.

I was happy with the opportunities the merger brought, and with how well the employees worked together and how seamlessly operations continued. In October 2012, EFS experienced another substantial growth opportunity when it acquired T-Chek Systems. Based in Minnesota, T-Chek was another payment processor that focused on the transportation industry; however, it had recently expanded to offer services to other industries. It was another complementary organization joining forces with EFS to create an even bigger company.

EFS was on a path for tremendous growth. I was surprised when Jimmy came to me and suggested we put EFS up for sale. He believed EFS's growth would be hampered by the affiliation with PFJ, and it was a seller's market. At first I was not in favor, but when I realized EFS could likely sell for over $1 billion, I knew he was right.

In business, everything is for sale if the price is right, so in May 2014, EFS was acquired by Warburg Pincus, a leading global private equity firm focused on growth investing. We would no longer own any of the card processing business. This legacy business, which continues to grow and expand, was sold again in July 2016 to WEX, Inc., a leader in the payment processing industry, and has grown the Ogden operation far bigger than ever before. Many former EFS employees still work for this new organization. The WEX name has replaced Flying J on the Ogden building, but I am proud that our former employees there continue to be part of a thriving company.

We used some of the proceeds from the sale of EFS to start our own DAF (donor-advised fund). This has proven to be another win for FJM, as the DAF has given us an ability to focus more on larger philanthropic efforts.

TAB

In 1998, Flying J formed Transportation Alliance Bank (TAB) to put ATM machines in truck stops for long-haul truckers to access cash on the road. By the time Flying J filed for bankruptcy in 2008,

TAB was strongly positioned in the financial world. It combined the security of a bank with the flexibility of a finance company for small and large companies throughout the country. TAB didn't feel many effects of Flying J's financial troubles, and in many ways was insulated from the bankruptcy process.

After the Pilot and Flying J merger, TAB became even more independent—it was no longer a bank with the sole mission to support Flying J. As such, it retooled its focus on providing banking services such as credit and debit card solutions, accounts receivable financing, equipment lending and leasing, and savings and investing options for thousands of small carriers and owner/operators.

The bank nearly doubled its assets by 2012, growing from $488 million to $838 million. But during 2012, TAB would unfortunately face a unique set of challenges—challenges that would pose substantial threats to the bank's operations and future.

In late 2011, TAB was presented with an opportunity to buy bulk affordable housing units that had been repossessed. The offer was irresistible—the bank could acquire the properties for pennies on the dollar. The plan was to rehabilitate the properties and lease to individuals with low credit scores, eventually giving them the opportunity to buy the property. The bank would get paid in full and would therefore potentially see an enormous financial windfall over time. But it wasn't as clear cut as it seemed.

In April 2012, the bank went through a standard safety and soundness exam. When the officers conducting the exam learned of the affordable housing project the bank had invested in, they seemed puzzled—right off the bat they questioned the portfolio's fit in an industrial bank. Within days the bank received a determination letter from the FDIC saying that it was an impermissible investment for the bank to own. TAB was given one month to get the asset off its books. FJ Management was forced to step in and buy the ailing asset for $53 million. We were eventually able to sell the affordable housing asset, but at a significant loss.

While the affordable housing asset was a financial loss for FJ Management and TAB, it wasn't the most significant problem the bank was experiencing at the time. On April 11, 2012, Chuck and I received a call about a troubling discovery at TAB that needed our attention right away. Chuck left immediately to learn more of the situation. Hours later I heard the news: there was compelling evidence that the bank president had created fraudulent loans totaling $8 million. I was in absolute shock and disbelief. I couldn't believe that Jeff Bell, one of our most trusted executives, would engage in this type of activity—it was completely outside of his character. We believed he was a top performer and he had our complete trust.

As the investigation unfolded throughout the following weeks, it became clear that Jeff had committed fraud. Unfortunately, he did not come clean with us until Chuck told him that we knew about what was going on. He was put on leave, but as more details came to light it looked worse and worse. We learned that he'd told an employee to fabricate invoice numbers, which made his actions a federal offense.

The discovered losses grew from $8 million to $20 million. The only good news for the bank was that regulators were working with us to clear up the situation. Meanwhile Chuck and I were struggling to understand why this president—someone we trusted, someone that we had brought on board—would do this. We also struggled knowing that this had happened under our watch.

Jeff Bell's employment was terminated in May 2012. He was later prosecuted in federal court and ordered to serve a 30-month sentence. In the end, this fraudulent activity had an enormous financial and emotional cost for the entire company—and for Chuck and me personally.

Chuck and the board worked tremendously hard to keep the bank afloat and to be certain we could get back on solid ground. It took time, but today, with just over 200 employees, TAB is the only original Flying J entity that still resides in the same Ogden, Utah, office space that we were in before the bankruptcy. With a growing number of people doing their banking online, TAB, which has no branches, continues to stay relevant in the banking business. TAB's primary business lines include asset-based revolving loans, accounts receivable financing, and equipment finance.

A New Opportunity

Principle: Building great relationships in life leads to opportunity.

s a holding company that held mostly petroleum assets, I
thought it was important that FJ Management build relationships in the petroleum industry. One person I greatly
enjoyed keeping up with was my cousin Mike Call, who was the
CEO of Maverik. By 2012, Maverik had grown to become one of the
largest convenience store chains across the western United States.
It had a long history with Call family ties.

In 1964, Reuel Call joined with his brother, my grandfather
Osborne, to form Caribou Four Corners, which would later become
Maverik. Though the worry was how the brothers would work
together, since they were both highly motivated deal makers with
entrepreneurial traits, this worry never came to a head, as Osborne
suddenly died of a heart attack just five months after they formed
Caribou Four Corners.

Jay and Teddy's first station in Willard, Utah, ca. 1960.

The fledgling corporation was left in a management crisis with Osborne's death. The retail end of the business was still being consolidated. Now working with two refineries, an expanding trucking and wholesale operation, and over 60 retail outlets, the firm was rapidly moving toward being a fully integrated petroleum enterprise. When Osborne died, Reuel wanted to keep the company intact. He suggested that Osborne's son, Jay (my father), take his father's place in Caribou Four Corners as a vice president and watch his newly widowed mother's interests in the company.

Jay worked with his uncle for three years and then went on to start Flying J. Osborne's side of the family continued to be a stockholder in the company until 1976, when their shares were bought out by Reuel's family.

By the time I met Mike, Reuel's grandson, in 2007, Maverik had been through three generations of family management and had a rich history. Reuel had been thrown out of management by his sons, who ran the company for many years. In 1999, the management passed to *their* sons, Reuel's grandsons, Mike and Brad Call. Under Mike and Brad's leadership, Maverik departed from its country-western theme. The brand became "Adventure's First Stop" to represent the high-energy outdoor activities popular in the Intermountain West. Stores were redesigned to be much larger, and interiors featured outdoor adventure elements such as illustrated wallpaper with outrageous landscapes, physical trees, and mannequins in adventurous poses. According to Brad, "When you walk into a Maverik, you're walking into the great outdoors!" By 2012, Maverik had more than 230 stores in 10 states and employed over 4,000 people.

Mike and I met periodically to catch up and discuss our family businesses, and I always thought that one day we might be partners. One of those meetings was in the fall of 2008, just a few months before Flying J's bankruptcy. Always on the lookout for an opportunity, I asked him if he were interested in merging the North Salt Lake Refinery and Maverik. I had always thought that the two entities would greatly complement and enhance each company's offerings. We decided the timing wasn't right and parted ways without discussing the potential merger further. But a seed had been planted and Mike knew that if he ever wanted to sell Maverik, I was interested.

In May 2012, I heard from Mike again—he wanted to meet for lunch and catch up. As I arrived at the New Yorker Restaurant in downtown Salt Lake, I had no idea that by the time the meal was over I would have in hand a new business opportunity. Mike did not come intending to talk to me about purchasing his company, but as we discussed our current situations he realized that FJ Management had money to invest and he told me he was considering selling Maverik. He wanted us to take a look since he was very interested in having Maverik stay in the Call family. He wanted to do a very quiet sales process so as not to upset his employees.

I was immediately intrigued. The timing was right. The bankruptcy was behind us and we had enough cash on hand to make an investment of this magnitude. Moreover, I knew that joining ranks with Maverik would be a significant win for our refinery. A merger would mean that the refinery would have a consistent customer to purchase its product. I knew that there were countless details and kinks to work out, but I was excited about the enormous opportunity the acquisition presented, so I was enthusiastically on board.

Mike and I and the FJM executive team spent the next two months devising a plan that would be mutually beneficial. Mike was excited about Maverik's potential and presented an aggressive growth plan he and his team had developed to expand the Maverik concept throughout the Intermountain West. The company expected to open 27 new convenience stores by March 2013. Most stores would be opened in the Las Vegas area, while Denver and North Dakota locations were also being considered.

Behind the scenes, Chuck and I were concerned that Maverik's growth potential, in so many different markets, wasn't quite as promising as what had been presented, but I remained committed to the deal. I told Mike that I would have an official offer to Maverik by July 26. We would present them with a plan for FJ Management to become majority owners.

The biggest hurdle to getting the deal finalized was agreeing on Maverik's long-term growth plan. We just didn't see the opportunity for growth that was presented, which impacted our financial offer. Mike and his executive team, on the other hand, were committed to following the growth plan they had developed. We went back and forth on the issue, and eventually decided to follow the growth plan cautiously.

In September, Chuck and I met with Mike and his cousin Brad, who was the executive vice president of Maverik, to present them with our official letter of intent. We had a blast going over the final details. It was so exciting to be bringing together our family's companies. We were all positive, upbeat, and reminiscent. We were all eager and ready to go.

Though we weren't excited about the growth plan, we *were* excited about the acquisition. The deal was nearly done by November 2012. This would be FJ Management's first major acquisition since recovering from the bankruptcy. We had worked out all the final details, including distribution, indemnifications, and employee exits, and were on track to get this deal signed by the end of the year.

While I was committed to the deal and believed it would be a great investment, I must admit I was starting to get cold feet, and so was Chuck. The long-term outlook for gasoline was a bit unclear, given the many efforts to market fuel-efficient cars, including electric vehicles, which I knew would impact not just Maverik but also our interests in Pilot Flying J. I didn't want to be so eager to complete the deal that I ignored the economic environment around us. But I also didn't want to let my fears of what could happen get in the way of this potential opportunity. We analyzed the numbers and decided the rewards outweighed the risk. We were going to move this deal forward.

Brad and Mike Call, and Crystal and Chuck Maggelet finalizing the Maverik deal on December 14, 2012.

In addition to purchasing the Call family stake in Maverik, there was a minority owner who owned 25 percent of the company. One of Mike's uncles had sold his shares years before, when he became disgruntled with his brothers, to a group of people willing to buy his stock without any rights. They had no seats on the board, no voting rights, and no ability to exit the shares or ask for any dividends. At some point I hoped we would have the opportunity to purchase these shares as well. Once the Maverik deal became public our opportunity came to talk to these shareholders. It was a cordial conversation with the stockholders' representative, Bill Whetton, and within a few hours we had a deal on the remaining 25 percent. They were happy even though they were paid a discounted price because of their minority ownership. It was a great return and outcome for them. When we met to finalize the deal, Bill made me feel so good when he told me he could now help his grandchildren with college.

On December 14, 2012, the deal was signed and closed. Together our team had made great progress, and only two and a half years after exiting bankruptcy not only had we paid off all our refinery debt, but we were also able to make our first acquisition, spending over $500 million to buy Maverik's 230 convenience stores located in 11 intermountain states. FJ Management was now officially the majority owner of Maverik—the business my grandfather and his brother had started together in 1964 had stayed in the Call family, and my father's dream of one day owning Maverik had come true. It felt great to again own a large retail fuel company.

During the first several weeks, the merger went as smoothly as I could have hoped for. Mike and I worked well together, and it was genuinely fun knowing that we had united our family businesses. Mike agreed to proceed slowly and cautiously with the growth plan.

We all wanted to ensure that if we opened new Maverik stores they would have every opportunity to succeed. I was extremely pleased with how the deal was coming together.

Most of our employees were just as pleased with the deal. Because Maverik had a solid brand in Utah, our decision to join forces with the company brought a new sense of confidence to many employees. For the first time since the bankruptcy, it was clear FJ Management was on solid ground. Employees and stockholders no longer viewed us as a fragmented organization made up of bits and pieces of several different companies.

But not everyone was excited about the merger, specifically employees at the North Salt Lake Refinery. They were upset that we had invested in Maverik. For several years running, the refinery had been the company's cash cow. Its performance was consistent and strong. They argued that FJ Management should be investing in the refinery, not in another company. I could see their point of view; however, I had hoped that they could also see ours. With Maverik part of our company, the refinery would have a consistent customer to provide product to. That was a huge benefit that would bolster the refinery for years to come.

Change in Leadership

The intent of our original deal was that the Maverik executive team would stay intact and sell a portion of their shares over the next five years. Only a few months after the acquisition, even though Mike and I worked well together, it was obvious it was going to be hard to keep the legacy management in place. Many of these executives had received large payouts and wanted to move on with their lives. We were the new owners and we were excited to impart our ideas and strategies to our new acquisition.

I felt as if Mike wanted a way out. He had committed to me that he would continue to lead Maverik for five years, but I could tell it was no longer any fun for him. I wanted to find a good solution for both of us. I approached a longtime Maverik board member and mentor of Mike's, Tom Welch, about the opportunity to step in for the next 18 months as CEO to transition the company to a new executive team. He was enthusiastic about the opportunity. I knew I had found the right person for the job. He understood Maverik inside and out and seemed to be on the same page with me regarding concerns and hopes for its future. Although it was not easy for Mike to leave Maverik, he felt comfortable that Tom would carry on his legacy. Over the next several months we purchased most of the remaining ownership of Maverik from the executives and Tom put together a new team of young, ambitious executives.

We have built nearly 100 more Maverik stores since we purchased the company. Our executive team and employees continue to get better and better at not only selling fuel, but providing a great in-store experience. In September 2016, three years after Tom Welch had agreed to an 18-month term as Maverik CEO, he became chairman of the board and Chuck took over as CEO. Chuck has continued to focus on growth, as well as bringing more operational oversight to Maverik. It is also great to have a family member running the company again.

It has also been exciting to be able to bring Flying J's ROSS POS system back to life. Since Pilot had decided not to use it in 2010, it had been mothballed. In 2015, when Maverik was looking for a better POS system for the stores, former Flying J executives now working at Maverik proposed bringing it back. The eight employees who had previously run ROSS, who were currently working at TCH, were recruited to come work at Maverik and bring the system back to life. We have since implemented a new version of ROSS, now called NITROSS. It is now the primary point-of-sale system at most of our Maverik stores.

One favorite experience of owning Maverik happened in January 2015. I surprised my 94-year-old grandmother, Verla Brown, with the honor of cutting the ribbon at a new Maverik store opening in her hometown of Rexburg, Idaho. I couldn't help but smile as she snipped the ribbon. It was exciting to think that the new store was on the very street where I learned to drive as a teen-ager while I was living in Idaho. It made me realize how far our family had come, considering that my grandparents didn't even have indoor plumbing on their farm until my mother's senior year of high school.

The grand opening of a new Maverik store in Rexburg, Idaho, in January 2015 featured Crystal's grandmother, Verla Brown, cutting the ribbon.

Val and Mike Call, and Crystal and Chuck at grand reopening of Maverik store in Afton, Wyoming, September 30, 2016.

Another very memorable event happened after we had owned Maverik for almost four years. We attended the grand reopening of the remodeled store in Afton, Wyoming, hosted by and Val and Mike Call (Reuel's son and grandson). Many of my father's siblings and my cousins also attended. This show of support for the Call family business where it all began made me proud and happy for all of us.

Moving On

*Principle: A positive attitude
wins in the end.*

I n 2010, when we merged with Pilot, I felt very comfortable that our Flying J brand would be in good hands. The Call and Haslam families both had strong values with many similarities. My dad's contemporary, Jim Haslam Sr., is still alive. In 1958, James started his company, Pilot Oil Corporation, in Gate City, Virginia. Just as my dad focused on developing petroleum properties in the West, James's focus was in the East. James later partnered with Marathon Oil just as Jay partnered with Conoco. Both companies are now run by the second generation of the families—Jimmy and me.

So it was shocking to hear on national news in April 2013 that the Pilot Flying J offices had been raided by the FBI. Their sales team had not been paying rebates due to their customers since 2006, before the merger, to the tune of several million dollars. The Haslam family was devastated and I was disappointed that the

Flying J brand had once again been tarnished. Now we even had a company catastrophe in common. Pilot Flying J was never charged, but was fined and put on probation. They also lost their whole sales team. Some were eventually sent to jail.

Jimmy and I had been through a lot together in eight years, yet Pilot Flying J was still thriving. With the future of petroleum demand at risk and companies selling for high prices, I was not surprised when I was approached by Jimmy about selling Pilot Flying J. At first I viewed it as an opportunity to reduce some of our petroleum holdings. When I learned that the sale price would be much lower than what I believed market value to be, my excitement died. Now I was faced with working a deal as a minority shareholder, acting as a responsible partner and friend without jeopardizing my fiduciary responsibility to our family business.

I knew the Haslams wanted to keep some ownership stake and stay somewhat involved, so they looked for a partnership in which they could remain a large part of the company and still exit at some point in the future. Even though *we* may not have been ready to exit Pilot Flying J, because we knew the Haslams' wishes and respected the Haslam family, we wanted to be good partners. So though it was tough to accept, we agreed to a staged buyout of our minority Pilot Flying J ownership to Berkshire Hathaway. We sold one-third of our Pilot Flying J stock in 2017 and will relinquish the rest in 2023. The legacy of Flying J–branded travel plazas owned by a Call family member will come to an end in 2023—44 years after it started. Knowing the stellar track record Warren Buffett has through Berkshire Hathaway, I feel my father's brand will be in good hands.

My family may no longer own the Flying J brand as my father knew it, but our family still has a strong, thriving business in the petroleum market through Maverik, which continues to expand.

In late 2012, when we were closing on the Maverik acquisition,

Owners of Pilot Flying J pictured in February 2018. Chuck and Crystal Maggelet (top row, left), Warren Buffet (bottom row, center), and several Haslam family members.

we made an offer on a high-rise office building in downtown Salt Lake City. By early 2013 we had moved most of the FJM staff to the new building and truly had a new beginning in a new space. Although the building at the time we purchased it had several outside tenants, it was my dream to move all our corporate offices for FJ Management, including Maverik and Crystal Inn, to this new building, and that dream came true in 2016. You can't miss the building, with tall red trim decorating the top of the 13th floor reading *Maverik Base Camp*. Since Maverik would be occupying most of the floors and is our public brand, it made sense to brand the building Maverik Base Camp after our Adventure's First Stop theme and to open our only nonfuel convenience store on the ground level. We no longer have outside tenants, and our building embodies our culture and history, complete with an FJM museum on the top floor.

Crystal at the current company headquarters, fall 2018.

Launching an Investment Division

After our creditors had been paid in full, in addition to our subsidiary companies we were left with $200 million cash. We used some of these funds to buy additional ownership in PFJ. We believed and hoped we would continue to have financial success, and we wanted to create diversification away from petroleum in our holding company, so we began investing in passive investments. As a closely held family organization, we first hoped we would find other family businesses to purchase. However, this was becoming a common theme and many private equity firms were looking for the same thing. They had much bigger sourcing teams and were willing to pay much higher prices to acquire companies. Other than buying Maverik, this strategy did not work very well due to the competition in the acquisition arena. We elected to hire staff to analyze minority direct and coinvestment opportunities, facilitate a cross-sector balanced public portfolio program, and make investments in various stage private equity funds. Over time we have invested in multiple asset classes over various industry sectors, and continue to pursue this investment thesis today as one of the core components of our mission statement, Building Value to Last.

Even with our Investment Division, since 75 percent of our family wealth is currently tied to petroleum-based products, and nobody knows when that commodity will become obsolete, we knew that building value to last would mean changing our business holdings from petroleum-based products to the next wave of demanded services. We were out to find another industry platform that we believed would grow to be as substantial in the next 20 to 30 years as our petroleum businesses are today.

We hired college interns to study the aging-population trend to look for potential opportunities for this growing market. They looked at mortuaries, senior living, and health care. We realized our existing skill set, which included real estate development and customer service, would serve us well in senior living. So by the end of 2017 we had invested in two entrepreneurial ground-up projects targeting the aging U.S. population.

Just as my grandfather and family did when they saw the need for supplying fuel to ranchers throughout the Four Corners region, we saw the need for affordable senior housing and services. Along with a new partner called WellQuest Living, we have leased three assisted living centers in Southern California and plan to break ground on two new projects in early 2019. We are also breaking ground on a GPS gerontology psychiatric hospital.

Giving Back

Since the conception of FJ Management, Chuck and I have tried to find ways to express our family's gratitude to the community that has supported us from Flying J's earliest days. We studied ways to give back to the Utah community, and decided that education would be our priority.

In 2013, FJ Management created the FJM Impact Fund to provide charitable giving to the community with a focus on improving education. We have donated over $2.5 million in annual scholarships to 12 educational institutions, and we continue to add schools to our program.

I am gratified and amazed at how our contributions make such a huge impact in the lives of families. As an example, I can remember being approached by a gentleman who asked me, "Do you remember my daughter? She had six kids under twelve years of age. Her husband was a child molester, so she left him and went to work at Big West to support her children. She was later a recipient of one of your scholarships." I remember thinking that she was a saint. People like that blow me away. I don't know how they do what they do.

Other scholarship recipients have written to us expressing their gratitude:

I was getting fuel and soda at a Maverik. I can't make this up. The phone rang and I was informed that I had received a scholarship. This resulted in life changing support in campus, as well as providing inspiration to push even harder in learning and developing.

The greatest gift I have ever received is the inspiration to make something of my life and be much more than previous expectations. I get to wake up every day, learn new ideas and pursue a higher lifestyle because of education. The way FJ Management has invested in my success inspires me to believe that we are capable of anything. I hope you can feel our gratitude.—Levi

Thank you for helping to assist me in accomplishing my goals to improve my education and my family's financial situation. I am a 38-year-old cancer survivor and mother of 5 children; 3 of my 5 children have mental health disabilities that have kept me out of the workforce for 10 years. For the last three years, my husband has been having difficulty retaining employment. This year, our last child was finally old enough that we were able to arrange things for me to be able to reenter the workforce and help support our family. But, with my 10-year lapse in work history, I was unable to find anyone willing to call me in for an interview. So, I have returned to school to increase my education and am finding many companies interested in hiring me once I complete my program.

This scholarship will help me do that and improve myself and my family's future while still being able to be there for my children at night. Thank you. Financially, I couldn't be going to school without the help that this scholarship provides.—Rebecca

In addition to promoting education, I give our employees the opportunity to contribute to organizations of their choice. We started a giving fund with a $300,000 annual budget. Any of our 5,500 employees can fill out a three-page application asking us for a financial contribution to a charitable organization they volunteer for and are passionate about. If approved, we donate to their cause in the employee's name. There are few restrictions on these requests, and we give to many different concerns, including health care, community organizations, and environmental causes.

We also found a way to give back to some of our former employees. Before the bankruptcy, 15 percent of the company stock was held in an ESOP program that had been frozen since the early 2000s. Once the bankruptcy was in motion the value went to zero for these stockholders. Our long-term employees, some of whom were laid off as a result of the bankruptcy, also now had no value in the stock they had accumulated throughout their careers. They had relied on this stock for their retirement. My goal was to bring the value back to at least where it was prior to entering bankruptcy. That goal was surpassed, as the stock value has since more than doubled its prebankruptcy value.

I wanted those who held stock to be paid out at the higher price. Many had written the stock off years before as a complete loss. We made a concerted effort to locate anyone who participated in the Flying J ESOP plan that had not received a payout. This amounted to about 350 people. It took extensive digging and research to locate these people. Some had married and changed their names; some had moved and left us without a forwarding address; and some had passed away, requiring us to find their next of kin. It took a legal team to fill out the necessary paperwork to release the funds to the rightful owners.

Some of the sweetest stories came from the surprise and heartfelt joy these former employees and their families felt when they were called and told that their ESOP payout was being held for them to claim. The payouts ranged from $5,000 to $150,000.

We heard numerous stories of how this money came at the most opportune time. One employee was losing his home and this money came at the right time to save it from foreclosure. Another had gone back to school to become a nurse, but with only one more semester left didn't know how she was going to pay for it. Yet another employee had just experienced a stroke and had been placed in a nursing home his family couldn't afford. His wife got power of attorney to claim his pension, which turned out to be $150,000, allowing her husband to stay in the home for the rest of his life. I am happy that most employees ended up holding their stock and that we were able to reward them for their time spent with Flying J.

Stories like these are what keep me going every day. As I get older I find more and more joy in giving back. Recently, because of our anticipated 2018 tax savings, we committed $10 million to increase most of our hourly workers' wages. This impacted over 3,000 employees. Comments such as, "This is life changing! I can quit my second job." and "Wow—thank you so much! This means so much to me." peppered our e-mails.

As a huge proponent of education, our Make the Grade program pays employees' children in grades 5 through 12 for every "A" awarded for a core class on their report card.

I have faith in people and am happy to financially help when I can. I have been blessed with an incredible life full of opportunity. So there is no better feeling for me than watching an employee or one of their children following through on their dream of higher education, or becoming independent learning to work at one of our properties. It is really what keeps me going. I love seeing the change in people's lives when they are able to take control of their own destiny.

Final Reflections

I've lived a life with a theme that was more about taking opportunities along the way then having goals and a direct path to get me there. The following attributes gave me the courage to jump in when an opportunity presented itself.

Self-Confidence

When my parents got divorced, my life changed dramatically and I did not know what our future would hold. Even though I was only 10, I learned that everything would be okay by just going along with whatever happens and making the best of a bad situation when necessary. My parents' divorce taught me to push through the tough times. It taught me that a circumstance might seem very bad when it happens, but worrying about it just takes time away from moving on and making it better. With time, almost everything works out if you keep trying and believe it will get better.

This lesson was reinforced throughout my childhood and as a young adult. I was fortunate to be given opportunities and challenges to overcome and was able to turn these events into something positive. My confidence grew as I saw the result of believing I could do something. It doesn't mean that I did not make mistakes; I made plenty of them. But I learned I could pick myself up and keep moving most of the time, always learning something along the way.

Taking on Challenges

Continuing to take chances and strive for something I wasn't certain I could accomplish added to my preparation for what came next in my life. I did not have any aspirations to go to Harvard Business School, but when the idea was presented I applied. At Harvard, I worked through many case studies that prepared me to evaluate situations, gather facts, and make a decision. This was critical when I became CEO of Flying J. Throughout the bankruptcy and restructuring of the company so much was going on I had to be willing to make quick decisions to keep the organization moving.

There's no doubt that the Flying J bankruptcy tested my stamina and grit. I remember thinking back to my mother's experience when she was starting her Diet Center franchises in Texas. I remember asking her where she got the guts to start up a business that she knew nothing about. Her reply was, "Nobody told me I couldn't do it, so I just did it." She kept this resolve when she went to open a bank account for her new business and the banker told her that it would not succeed because Texans didn't like outsiders. I felt a kindred spirit by her reply of, "Then I guess I will show you!"

Surrounding Yourself with the Best People

Some would argue that leading Flying J through bankruptcy was beyond my abilities. They were correct. It was a huge undertaking and having smart, capable people around me was critical to my success. Being able to accept and ask for help does not mean you are weak. It means you recognize that others may be better qualified for certain things than you are. My career has been possible because of the individuals who have worked by my side. Not only at work but also at home I've been helped greatly. On more than one occasion I'd find the mom who did hair best and ask them to do my daughters' hair. I wanted my girls' hair to look great for special events and I knew I was not the person for the job. Whether at home or at work, one of the secrets to my success has been to surround myself with the best people I can find to help me out and keep me on track.

Finding Balance Over a Lifetime

When I became president and CEO of Flying J, I made the decision to put life as I knew it on hold and work until we were out of bankruptcy and our creditors were paid. I believed our family business had good assets and that working one day at a time we could do it. I knew that my home life would be impacted, but I hoped that Chuck and the kids would understand. I wasn't the only one impacted—my family and our employees made sacrifices along the way as well.

Finding and maintaining balance in one's life is not easy, and I believe cannot be measured day by day. Instead, my belief is that balance is accomplished over a lifetime. I remember being a young mother with four children trying to have it all. I'd look at my life and think that everything was great. I had beautiful children. Our holidays and vacations were memorable. I had dinner on the table most nights. I was the mom I always wanted to be—and I still kept one foot in the door at Flying J and Crystal Inn. It seemed as if I had it all, yet I wasn't completely happy. I remember thinking to myself, "What is your problem? This is balance."

When the bankruptcy hit and I became president and CEO, the exact opposite happened. I threw myself into the business 100 percent, sacrificing my family and home life. Though I didn't have much of a choice, I began to realize that making short-term sacrifices, whether it be at home or work, was key to long-term fulfillment. I couldn't balance every single day, but I could find balance over a lifetime. For me, my success will be measured very far in the future, when I can look back and feel that I led a balanced life that included a great family and a productive career, and that I left a positive mark on the world because of the things I accomplished and gave back.

Choosing Your Partner Wisely

Another very important part of individual success if you choose to have a partner is choosing the *right* partner. I am absolutely positive that without a person like Chuck in my day-to-day life my story would have been very different. He is my life partner and has supported me for 25 years. Of course there have been ups and downs in our relationship as we've maneuvered through raising four kids and running large businesses together.

Chuck and I have similar entrepreneurial roots. While my family was building a fuel business in the West, Chuck's was building a bus company in Maryland. In 1919, Chuck's grandfather Joseph Francis Restivo and his brothers established the Baltimore Motor Coach Co. in Baltimore. During World War II, my grandfather and great-uncles provided their crop planes for the war effort. Chuck's grandfather and great-uncles dedicated their buses to transporting defense workers to various sites around Baltimore. In 1979, Joseph and his brothers sold the company. Chuck certainly understands the value and sacrifice behind a family business. And luckily he is ethical, grounded, confident, and hardworking.

Over the past few years I have received many awards and accolades for heading up the restructuring of Flying J and paying back creditors. Throughout it all, Chuck, my silent partner, was in the background and typically overlooked. I know this must not be easy, yet Chuck has never complained or done anything to undermine my success.

I remember how frustrated I was when the word around town was that "Jay Call bought his daughter a hotel chain for her wedding." Chuck was put in the same position as he worked tirelessly behind the scenes to help organize FJ Management. I seem to be the one always in the limelight. I know Chuck hasn't received his fair share of accolades, nor do I think he wants to be in the public eye. Still, to set the record straight, Chuck is a smart, very capable business partner who has made a huge contribution to the success of our family enterprise. He adds value to whatever he touches. He's currently the CEO and "Chief Adventure Guide" at Maverik.

Maintaining a Family Legacy

Keeping our family business was important to my father. Occasionally, as the business became larger, he would be asked why he didn't take it public or cash out, especially later in his life when he was not involved day to day. His answer was always the same. He believed the company was not only there for our family, but also for the many other families we employed. His wishes continue to be my wishes, and now I understand more than ever why he felt this way. I am often told that my father would be very proud. I will never know for sure if this is true, but I am very proud to continue the family legacy.

Owning and keeping a family business adds a layer of pressure and responsibility on our children that other kids don't normally encounter. Thad and I were taught, and have taught our own children, that just because you come from wealth does not make you any better than anyone else. If you fail, you will fail like anyone else; and if you succeed, it was your achievement like anyone else. You are not superior to anyone just because of your net worth. Chuck and I have tried to raise our children like a typical middle-class family. We don't have or need the finest cars, clothes, and homes. Yes, we have spoiled them with experiences like travel, but at home we want them to be able to relate to their peers.

We have made a concerted effort to downplay wealth in our family life. I remember too well how I felt about the kids I traveled with on Semester at Sea. I had no interest in the kids that were spoiled or felt entitled. We have taught our children that it is more important to have people respect you for what you accomplish than to rely on family wealth to create false confidence. As long as you know you are working hard and doing your best, you will be respected at least by those who really know you.

Chuck and I have been asked numerous times if we are grooming the next generation to continue the family business. The third generation consists of six, ages 18 to 33. They are well educated and industrious, and there would be a place in our companies for any of them. Our kids over 18 are encouraged to come as observers to our board meetings and stay informed about the activities of the family business. We hope to continue to have a family member leading our businesses, but we also realize that to have long-term success we will need the best leader at the top, which may or may not be a family member. With that said, the next generation is being trained to be stewards of our business and will be welcomed into the companies after meeting three requirements: a college education, outside work experience, and a sincere desire to be a part of the family enterprise.

FJ Management employees on a company trip to celebrate 50 years in Jackson Hole, Wyoming, September 2018.

Thad's adult children, Whitney and Tyson, attend company board meetings but have found other passions to be involved in. Our four children are also pursuing passions and educations of their own.

Our oldest and only son, Drew, graduated from the University of Miami with a bachelor's degree in political science. He currently works at Zions Bancorporation, encouraging its employees to get more involved in local and federal government. Lexi is currently completing her bachelor's degree at USC in gerontology, studying the geriatric concerns of the nation's baby boomers and potential solutions to the problems facing that aging population. Our twins, Erica and Hailey, are both freshmen at Notre Dame.

It is clear to our kids that I hope our family business can continue with their generation, but I hope they also know they need to live their own lives and pursue their own dreams, whatever those may be.

Epilogue

My life has had many twists and turns over the past few months that are leading me not only to the end of writing this book, but to the end of this chapter in my life. In early June 2018, I received the Lifetime Achievement Award as part of Ernst and Young's Entrepreneur of the Year Awards for the Utah region. It was an honorary award that I did not compete for. All my immediate family and several long-term employees attended the awards ceremony. It was a highlight of my business career to date. When I stood to give my acceptance speech, the audience rose for a standing ovation. I was very humbled, since the audience was made up of many ambitious and successful entrepreneurs. I was on a high. In November 2018, at the national Ernst and Young event, I was presented the Family Business Award.

On June 9, 2018, my brother Thad fell and fatally hit his head. Only a few weeks after my brother's celebration of life, our first

Coworkers, family, and friends at the Ernst and Young Entrepreneur of the Year awards gala, June 2018.

child, Drew, was married and we happily welcomed another member, Monet, into our family. Only a few weeks later another big event occurred when Chuck and I dropped our youngest twin girls, Hailey and Erica, off at college and became empty nesters.

Celebrating our 25th wedding anniversary on October 23, 2018, Chuck and I have been asked how we have been able to make our marriage work so well, especially working together professionally. Since neither of us had been married before we had no expectations, and since we waited until after graduating from college, we were already aware of what our professional dreams were and how willing we were to accomplish them. Being relatively committed and relatively goal oriented we knew we would just make it work. Over time we have come to accept that to have a successful business-marriage partnership we will typically agree 65 percent of the time, compromise 20 percent, and most importantly realize that we are never going to agree 15 percent of the time, so we just work around it. With that understanding we are looking forward to many anniversaries to come.

Yet again, I plan to embrace these changes and take the advice my father once gave me when I asked him what his business goals had been. He said, "Every morning I would look in the mirror and ask myself if I was going to work because I loved it. Since the answer was always yes, I didn't have to think about an alternative for the foreseeable future." I will also continue to strive to do what makes me happy while hopefully working to continue Building Value to Last.

Acknowledgments

One of my biggest fears in writing a book is that I offend someone in the process or don't give credit where credit is deserved. The fact is, if you're reading this there's a good chance your name should rightly be included in a list of acknowledgments. Because of all the people who have crossed my path these past 54 years and who have made a difference in my life, that list would likely fill up an entire book on its own, so I hope that you'll forgive its absence here.

I would like to take this space to provide special thanks to a few people that helped this book become a reality by offering their personal insights of events, reviewing my drafts, or providing their support and encouragement:

Tamra Call
Whitney Call
Tyson Call
Lars Call
Teddy and Rod Chamberlain
Chuck Maggelet
Drew Maggelet
Lexi Maggelet
Erica Maggelet
Hailey Maggelet
Sharon and Larry Anderson
Brett Bailey
Jim Baker
Scott Clayson
Gina Dalton

Mark Farmer
Karen Goodlow
Fred Greener
Josh Grotstein
Dustin Hancock
John Hillam
Boyd Hunter
Rob Inkley
Ted Jones
Andre Lortz
Vanesa Martinez
Jon Peterson
Richard Peterson
Stan Vincent
Sheri Widerburg

Index

Note: **Boldfaced** page numbers indicate photographs.